A STUDEN
TO TEACHIN

6.0

A Student's Guide
to Teaching Practice

ALAN COHEN, M.A., M.Ed.
*Lecturer in Education, University of Durham,
Institute of Education, Durham*

and

NORMAN GARNER, M.Ed.
*Formerly Head of the Education Department, Ethel Wormald Day
College of Education, Liverpool*

UNIVERSITY OF LONDON PRESS LTD

ISBN 0 340 15462 4

First published 1963

Third edition copyright © 1971 Alan Cohen and Norman Garner
Third impression 1975

University of London Press Ltd
St Paul's House, Warwick Lane, London EC4P 4AH

Printed and bound in England by
Hazell Watson & Viney Ltd, Aylesbury, Bucks

Contents

CONTENTS

Acknowledgments

The authors wish to acknowledge the assistance and advice given by their colleagues in colleges of education. Thanks are due to: Miss J. Rintoul, B.A., *Lecturer in English, C. F. Mott College of Education*; Mr. G. J. Gurney, B.A., *Former Principal, Malayan Teachers' Training College*; Mr. J. Kennedy, M.A., *Senior Lecturer in History, Stafford College of Education*; Mr. P. Townsend, B. A., *Lecturer in Geography, Ethel Wormald College of Education;* Mr. L. Cohen, M.A., *Senior Lecturer in Sociology, Edge Hill College of Education;* Mr. A. Dawson, B.Sc., *Principal Lecturer in Science, Edge Hill College of Education*; Mr. R. E. Wilson, B.Sc., *Lecturer in General Science, Edge Hill College of Education*; Mr. J. E. Wilde, *Carnegie Dip. in Physical Education, Principal Lecturer in Physical Education, Edge Hill College of Education*; Mr. E. Wright, *Carnegie Dip. in Physical Education, Lecturer in Physical Education, Edge Hill College of Education*; and Mr. T. W. Eason, M.A., *Principal Lecturer in Education, Edge Hill College of Education.*

Thanks are also due to the following for permission to use extracts which appear in the text:

Mr. K. Wormald, O.B.E., B.A., *Solicitor to the National Union of Teachers*; The Schoolmaster Publishing Co. Ltd.; Her Majesty's Stationery Office; Methuen & Co. Ltd.; J. M. Dent & Sons, Ltd.; the Oxford University Press; The Epworth Press; Longmans, Green & Co. Ltd.; and the Macmillan Company, New York.

The authors would also like to record their appreciation of the great assistance given by Mr. J. S. Ross, C.B.E., M.A., B.Sc., who read the whole of the manuscript and made many valuable suggestions.

Foreword

I feel it an honour to be asked to write a foreword to *A Student's Guide to Teaching Practice* by Alan Cohen and Norman Garner, which appears opportunely at a time when there is a drive to produce teachers and still more teachers. The authors, who know well the problems and difficulties that beset the path of the beginner in teaching, have much sound advice to offer him. There can be no colleges of education which fail to regard teaching practice as of the highest importance; yet it is perhaps true to say that, with the present desirable emphasis on the intellectual and personal development of the student, there is less than there used to be in the older colleges of education on the craftsmanship in teaching. As one who at an earlier stage bore the time-honoured but now discarded title of Master of Method I welcome the stress on method, craftsmanship and artistry that is to be found here. I would very specially commend what is said about painstaking preparation of lessons and the compiling of notes. In my long experience of teacher training I always found that thorough and detailed preparation, not only of matter but also of method, set forth in orderly notes, paid handsome dividends; and that it was the most promising young teachers who took the greatest pride in compiling note books that were their own very valuable manuals of teaching practice, as well as a joy for their Master of Method to behold. Now that I am relegated to the inferior status of examiner I keep stressing, possibly *ad nauseam* in my visits to colleges of education, the importance of careful preparation recorded in orderly notes. To those who, mistakenly I think, regard such a doctrine as a mere survival of an outworn training college tradition I would say that if it is old fashioned it is none the less sound, and indeed that real craftsmanship in teaching cannot be otherwise acquired. It is because I am happy to find this view so fully shared by two of my younger colleagues that I have special pleasure in commending their book not only to students but also to those who supervise and guide their work in schools.

J. S. Ross,
C.B.E., M.A., B.SC.
Former Principal, Westminster Training College.

Introduction

Every year, in colleges of education in Great Britain, thousands of students are sent out into schools to practise the art of teaching. After many years of study in a variety of schools, they find themselves as absolute beginners in the profession they have chosen, and in which many of them will spend a considerable part of their lives. Nothing accentuates the realisation of this fact more than their first teaching practice.

Many educationists believe that the student's school practice is the most vital part of his professional training. Few would challenge the contention that the student's practice in schools should be the focal point of all the other training he receives. It is on this occasion that he has his first opportunity to put into application some of the psychology, methods and principles he has learned theoretically in lecture rooms.

As a factor in the scheme of education in schools and colleges the ramifications of school practice are extensive —more extensive than is often realised. A great deal of preliminary administrative work is involved in placing students in different schools before the practice begins, and much of the success of this organisation depends upon the harmonious relationship and understanding which is built up between the head teachers and their staffs and the college authorities. At present, nearly eighty thousand students in colleges of education spend an average of four weeks practising in schools. Soon this number will rise to

100,000. A conservative estimate of their influence is that, in every year, they will come into contact with:

8,000 College of education lecturers
40,000 Schools
40,000 Head teachers
100,000 Classes
150,000 Class teachers
4,000,000 Pupils

The problems of teaching practice deserve to be treated in their own right.

There are many hints and suggestions concerning lesson writing and planning to be found in a variety of admirable text books on Teaching Method. These invariably relate school practice to the overall professional training in Philosophy, Psychology and General Methods given to the student. This volume will not add to the number of such books; it is designed to draw attention particularly to the many practical and human problems encountered whenever a student faces a class, in fact from the moment he enters a school. It is intended to show the realistic application of the professional training that the student receives in college. It is a codification and extension of the kind of advice and instructions which are often given verbally, or in summarised form, before each school practice. In short, the book is directed to the student about to embark on any of his practices, and is designed to prepare him for the minutiae of detail that make up the daily work of the class teacher—work which will soon become a part of the student's life.

CHAPTER ONE

Initial Considerations

The Student as an Apprentice

It has become commonplace in modern educational theory to associate learning with doing. Most students are aware of the implication of the phrase: 'the curriculum is to be thought of in terms of activity and experience rather than of knowledge to be acquired and facts to be stored.'* At least these words suggest that we focus our attention on the children themselves as learners, as well as on the methods used to educate them. Children learn by becoming engaged in meaningful activity, and by experiencing and doing they realise the purpose of that activity.

In the school practice situation the principle of learning by doing still holds true. The student learns the practical application of his art by his own meaningful activity—in the classroom. Thus the most important purpose of teaching practice is to help the student to learn his job.

Fleming uses the word 'craftsman' to describe the teacher's skill. 'Teachers are craftsmen in their concern with the material under their hand. They are cognisant of the variety and the uniqueness of their charges and aware of the personal and social processes by which modifications can be wrought. They are craftsmen also

* *The Primary School* Report of the Consultative Committee of the Board of Education, 1931 (H.M.S.O.).

in their interest in the stimulation they offer—its content in terms of activity and knowledge, and the materials of instruction through which it can take perceptible shape.'*

A craftsman becomes a skilled technician by the slow process of acquiring specific skills and patiently accumulating knowledge about his medium. The student, particularly while on school practice, is an apprentice to his craft, and the deliberate use of the words 'slow' and 'patiently' must indicate that the process of becoming a teacher, in the real sense of the word, takes a considerable time. The student should approach this period of 'practical learning' with the spirit of the apprentice: someone who is aware of his limitations and inexperience and eager to profit and learn his craft from the advice and help of those who are already qualified.

The Student as an Experimenter

The student should always be prepared to experiment.

(a) Teaching is an individual art; no two teachers use identical methods or are alike in their approach. The student must try to realise his talents and potentialities from the beginning so that he can use them to his advantage. He has to fuse his own personality with his needs as an educator.

(b) There are many well-tried methods of teaching. The degree of success with which these general methods can be applied will depend largely on the personality of the person using them. The student should experiment with these to find out which work best for him.

* C. M. Fleming *Teaching: A Psychological Analysis* (Methuen) p. 153.

(c) One does not learn how to teach children from a text book alone. The school gives the opportunity for the student to gain first-hand knowledge of the children he teaches. It also gives him a chance to discover for himself the material and equipment he has at his disposal and the possibilities and extent of its use.

(d) Every teaching situation is unique because the participants are themselves unique and individual. Theory cannot provide the answer to every contingency. Teaching demands versatility and the ability to respond to the unpredictable quickly and effectively. In this sense the general methods the student is taught need interpreting in terms of human relations in the classroom. The student develops his skill through 'reasoned' trial and error methods, guided by the general principles and methods with which he is familiar.

The Student and the School

The student must realise that as a beginner he is a long way from being a skilled teacher and is, therefore, in need of guidance. This makes the head teacher's responsibility for the student and to the children in his school of immediate importance.

'One point we must get established. As long as you are in that particular school, you are under the authority of the head. You may feel that his conception of education is old-fashioned and some of his rules and regulations of questionable merit. Never mind. He is in charge. Even when he wants things done in a way which does not tally with what you have been told by your lecturers, it is his word that must be obeyed. And your lecturers will wish you to recognise that authority while you are practising your craft in that school.'*

The apprentice potter has clay as his medium. If he makes a mistake, he ruins his efforts but little harm is done because the material is expendable. The student, however, is working with precious, unexpendable material. Mistakes he will certainly make, but he should be aware that his material may suffer under his hands. He must therefore strive to make as few mistakes as possible.

* K. M. Roach *I Want to Teach* (U.L.P.) p. 27.

CHAPTER TWO

The Preliminary Visit

Most colleges of education provide their students with an opportunity to visit the schools before teaching practice begins.

The Object of the Preliminary Visit

(a) To obtain the information and materials required to enable the student to teach.

(b) To meet the head teacher and staff of the school.

(c) To meet the class teacher and the children.

(d) To assimilate the atmosphere of the school.

For the convenience of readers, advice and instructions on how to use the preliminary visit profitably have been classified under two headings:

1. What to look for; and
2. What to bring back.

1. WHAT TO LOOK FOR

Schools vary greatly in their general approach to the task of teaching children. They differ in method, organisation and policy. During this preliminary visit the student should notice the general way in which the school is run.

While it is better for him not to copy any other teacher, it is better for him not to try swimming against the stream. The approach must be adjusted to fit in with, or at least to accept, the prevailing climate, which it is beyond his power to alter.

Method of the School

Some schools foster and encourage competition, others co-operative behaviour. Some are restrictive and authoritarian while others encourage freedom of expression. Any attempt to impose an alien method on any well-established and efficient system will be unlikely to succeed and may undermine the achievements of the prevailing order.

Class Teacher's Manner

The work of the class may deteriorate if the student's attitude is diametrically opposed to that of the class teacher. The student with integrity and the courage of his own convictions should be patient and realise that the opportunity for the development of his own ideas will come after qualification. Absolute non-conformity and radicalism are inappropriate in school practice.

Method of Work—Exercise Books

The class teacher's manner will be reflected in the way he deals with the exercise books. They will reveal the standard he sets, the methods of marking and correction he uses, and the way he exploits the information provided by the children in their written work. Studying and marking exercise books is not an 'extra' teaching duty, but an essential part of the educative process, and should be treated by the student with the importance accorded it by most class teachers.

Routine Organisation

The average class teacher would claim that it takes about three months to get a class to do things the way he wants. In other words, it takes this length of time to establish routine organisation. Teachers have their own ways of distributing, collecting and checking equipment, sharpening pencils, etc. Failure to consider these matters often results in the waste of good teaching time.

The class teacher's methods of organisation will have been evolved in the light of his experience and superior knowledge of the particular children he teaches. The student possesses neither this knowledge of the children, nor the time that is available to the class teacher to get to know all that can be known about each particular child. For reasons of economy of effort and time alone he would be well advised to perpetuate the established order and routine throughout his period of practice. Studying the routine and class organisation requires close observation because the most effective methods are often the least obvious.

2. WHAT TO BRING BACK

Schemes of Work and other Details of the Class

The student should bring back Schemes of Work, with necessary details, in all the subjects he is expected to teach. The details will include the following:

(a) *Name of the class.* The significance of names given to classes is not always apparent to the uninitiated. 'Class I' could be the youngest or the oldest in the school. Again, to avoid possible adverse psychological effect on the children, many schools, more so secondary than primary, use their own order of letters (other than A, B, C, D) to indicate the stream of a class. As these letters do not of themselves give a newcomer to the school any information, care must be taken to find out just what these letters mean.

(b) *Size of the class.* The number of children in a class makes a difference to the organisation and presentation of the various curriculum activities.

(c) *Average age of the children.* Lessons with a similar content cannot be given to children of very different ages. The average age of the children affects the content and approach of the work to be tackled.

(d) *Stream of the class or ability of the children.* Many students imagine that work prepared for an 'A' stream can be given, with little modification, to a 'D' stream. This is a negation of all the principles of individual differences in ability. The work must be adjusted to the ability of the children.

(e) *Sex of children.* Students must take into account the differences in physique, interests and attitudes between the sexes, particularly with older children.

(f) *Length of lessons.* Account has to be taken of the children's span of attention and the need to occupy all of their time in purposeful activity. Lessons may extend over more than one time table period.

(g) *Accounts of pupils' previous knowledge in all subjects.* This information is most valuable. It is vital that students should know where to begin each activity. Repetition of work already learned can be disastrous, unless designed as controlled revision. New knowledge should, as far as possible, be linked with knowledge that is already familiar, to make the new learning more coherent and meaningful.

(h) *Equipment available.* Amount and quality of equipment varies greatly from school to school. The student will wish to verify that the school possesses the equipment he requires, and he will want to acquaint himself with all the facilities offered by the school.

(i) *General facilities of the school.* School building is not standardised, and therefore buildings vary. Size of cupboards, display space, adjustability of blackboards, even the size and shape of the classrooms differ greatly. Schools also vary in provision of sinks, power points, water supply, etc.

Seating Plan and Particulars of the Children

All students are advised to prepare a plan of the classrooms in which they are going to teach, with—if possible—the names of the children shown in their places. It is a tremendous advantage if these names can be learned before the school practice begins. This plan should be supplemented with the following information:

(a) 'Whether or not the arrangement of tables, desks and children is deliberate and fits into a scheme.

(b) Information about children who present special problems, e.g. short-sighted, hard of hearing, etc.

(c) Information about children who present unusual behaviour problems, e.g. maladjusted, mentally or physically handicapped, etc.

Time Tables

(*a*) Exact time tables will be required for the student's use in preparing his work.

(*b*) Copies of these will usually be required by the supervisor and the college authorities in order to enable them to organise their visits economically.

(*c*) Students should record and be prepared for half classes, sets for special activities and, on some occasions, for the regular administrative and other interruptions with which all schools are plagued, e.g. milk deliveries, the collecting of savings and dinner money, etc.

Text Books

(*a*) These are necessary to prepare the work adequately according to the schemes of work provided.

(*b*) The student should obtain one copy of every set he will use.

(*c*) He should sign for these books, look after them and, on completion of his school practice, RETURN them.

CHAPTER THREE

Preparation of Schemes of Work

The scheme of work will indicate the amount of ground a student is likely to cover during his stay in the school. It is a survey of the work he intends to cover, and it allows him to plan and develop those particular curriculum experiences which he may feel will require more time and attention in preparation. The scheme also helps the student to provide continuity in the work and sequence in the learning process.

What to include in a Scheme of Work

The scheme of work will contain information about the children in the class. Modern educational theory stresses the importance of the recognition of the individual differences that exist in children and the need to take account of them and plan for them. No two children are the same; no two classes are the same. The student should bear in mind that he is teaching children, as well as teaching subjects, and that the needs of the children will determine the actual content of what is taught.

Thus the scheme of work will contain details of the average age of the class to be taught, the name and stream or group of the class taught, and the sex of the children.

A scheme of work should contain an account of the class's previous knowledge. What the children already know will determine what they can effectively learn.

New knowledge should be related to existing knowledge and, therefore, what the children have already experienced in their learning must be known to the teacher if he is to be effective. He should not leave gaps in the children's knowledge, nor assume that they know material which they have, in fact, not learnt. A well-planned scheme of work will avoid unnecessary and boring repetition with the risk of losing the children's interest and causing disciplinary problems.

The student should take into account the number and duration of the lessons he will teach. This might vary from four to twenty or more in a week, and from twenty-five minutes to one hundred and forty minutes.

The student should be aware of the total subject matter he is likely to teach during his practice period and the most suitable sequence of presentation. Equipped with this information, the overall aim for the whole scheme of work should become clear. The scheme of work is often divided, for the sake of convenience and systematic development, into weekly or fortnightly stages.

An important principle of the learning process is that children learn through multi-sensory experiences. The whole array of visual aids, films, special equipment, books, etc. contribute to their experience. The student should make full use of all the equipment the school has to offer, and this should be considered when he is searching for interesting ways of teaching.

In short, then, the following information should be included in a scheme of work:

(a) Particulars of the children: age, sex, ability, stream (if appropriate).

(b) Previous knowledge of the class.
(c) Number and duration of the lessons.
(d) Aim of the scheme.
(e) Subject-matter and sequence.
(f) Equipment: materials, books, apparatus and aids.

The scheme is not intended to prescribe in detail the student's activities during the whole school practice. Its main purpose is to help to clarify his thought, and guide his subsequent detailed preparation of the various curriculum areas he will tackle. In many cases modifications in the amount and content of material will be made in the light of further knowledge of the individual differences which exist in the class. It is usually recommended that a scheme of work in each subject to be taught should be prepared before teaching practice begins. This is included in the lesson notes file, at the head of the section of lesson notes on the subject.

Here is a useful formal layout of a scheme of work:

Subject:
Particulars of Children: (age, sex, ability, stream, number in class)

Subject-matter: (a) Lessons—number and duration
              (b) General Aim of the Scheme
              (c) Previous Knowledge
              (d) Scheme: Week I
                         Week II
                         Week III
                         Week IV

Books and Equipment needed: (materials, aids, apparatus)

Some Specimen Schemes

Example A

SUBJECT: Art and Craft

PARTICULARS OF CHILDREN: Age 10+
           Sex: Mixed
           Form: Third-year class
           Number: 33

SUBJECT-MATTER:

(a) *Lessons*—1 lesson of 60 mins. per week for 4 weeks.

(b) *General Aim*—To give the children practice in modelling and painting through learning how to construct glove puppet heads.

(c) *Previous Knowledge*—Experience in the use of plasticine, making strip papier-mâché models of animals, painting and varnishing papier-mâché models, making match-box and paper-sculpture glove puppets.

SCHEME OF WORK:

Week 1 Lesson 1

Modelling—high relief of head in plasticine.

Instruction by the teacher on how to construct features on smooth base.

Children complete model of head.

Week 2 Lesson 2

Constructing papier-mâché skin. Papier-mâché laid on model piece by piece. 7 layers required. Alternating colours of paper. Introduced by teacher demonstration.

Week 3 Lesson 3

Plasticine removed from hardened papier-mâché skin. The head-shape constructed with crushed paper. Back of head constructed with papier-mâché. Modelling completed.

Week 4   *Lesson* 4

Painting the papier-mâché model in poster colour. Varnishing when dry. The adding of hair, eye-brows, etc.

APPARATUS:

Plasticine, modelling tools, paste, paste-brushes, scissors, tissue paper (2 colours), petroleum jelly, paint, paint-brushes, varnish, brushes, newspaper, wool.

Example B

SUBJECT: General Science

PARTICULARS OF CHILDREN: Age: 11+
                              Sex: Mixed
                              Form: Fourth-year class
                              Number: 41

SUBJECT-MATTER:

(*a*) *Lessons*—2 lessons of 35 mins. per week for 3 weeks.

(*b*) *General Aim*—To introduce children to the concept of heat in as many practical ways as possible.

(*c*) *Previous Knowledge*—Little previous formal instruction. Scheme is designed to draw upon previous knowledge from every-day living, and to examine this in a scientific way.

SCHEME OF WORK:

Week 1   *Lesson* 1   *Temperature*

(*a*) Experiencing different temperatures—ice, snow, radiator, fire, hot and cold water, etc.

(*b*) How temperature is measured—reference to clinical thermometers in hospitals, every-day knowledge of illness, correlation with the geography lessons children have had on arctic, temperate and tropical lands.

27

Week 1 *Lesson* 2 *Temperature—Measurement*

(*a*) The story of Fahrenheit, the German glass-blower.

(*b*) Simple account of how the Fahrenheit thermometer works.

Activities—measuring body temperature; hot and cold water in taps.

Week 2 *Lesson* 3 *How Heat Travels—Conduction*

Experimental lesson—hot poker in water, poker loses heat, water gains. Discussion—insulation, lagging of pipes, tropical kit in hot lands, woollen underclothing, tea-cosy, thermos flask.

Week 2 *Lesson* 4 *How Heat Travels—Radiation*

Warming hands in front of the fire. How does the heat get from the fire to hands? How does bread get toasted? The sun's rays.

Experiment—with black paper and white paper. Black paper is hotter than white paper when both are warmed. Black absorbs heat; white reflects.

Week 3 *Lesson* 5 *Effects of Heat—Change of State*

Melting—heat makes many things melt: ice, butter, wax, sugar, lead, etc.

Experiment—Separating salt from sand.

Difference between solid and liquid state.

Difference between dissolving and melting.

Week 3 *Lesson* 6 *Effects of Heat—Boiling and Evaporation*

Heat can make liquids boil. Steam and cooling of steam in air.

Experiment—with piece of glass held over steam.

Condensation.

Saucer of water slowly dries up. Wet pavements. Wet clothes. Evaporation.

APPARATUS:

Gas ring, metal and wooden spoons, water container, bone knitting needles, metal and glass rods, teapot and tea-cosy, thermometers, thermos, black and white paper, ice, wax, butter, sugar, salt, sand, metal trays, piece of glass, mirrors.

Example C

SUBJECT: Mathematics

PARTICULARS OF CHILDREN: Age: 13+
Sex: Boys
Form: 3B
Number: 30

SUBJECT-MATTER:

(a) *Lessons*—5 lessons of 60 mins. per week for 4 weeks.

(b) *General Aim*—To apply knowledge of speed, time and distance, acquired in previous learning, and to demonstrate the uses to which such knowledge can be put in the experiences of every-day life.

(c) *Previous Knowledge*—Children have had many experiences of the concepts of time, speed and distance: the contents of the scheme are of real interest to them already. The teacher seeks to organise this interest and examine the mathematics underlying the work.

SCHEME OF WORK:

Week 1   *Title—Time tables*
    Lesson 1 Bus time tables—activities.
          2 Railway time tables—activities.
          3 Airway time tables—activities.
          4 Ships' schedules.
          5 Continental holiday itineraries (land, sea, air).

Week 2   Title—Records (speed, time and distance)
   Lesson   6 Stop watch activities (over 110 yards)
          7 Athletic records—swimming, running.
          8 Land, sea and air speed records.
          9 Motor cars—rates of speed, acceleration.
         10 Animals—speeds (horse, greyhound, racing pigeons, etc.).

Week 3   Title—Scientific Measurement
   Lesson 11 Speed of light.
         12 Speed of sound (radio, telegram, sound barrier etc.).
         13 Icebergs, echo-soundings, radar.
         14 Seismology, earthquakes, oil seismology.
         15 Space travel—rockets, projectiles, velocity, centrifugal force.

Week 4   Title—General Knowledge (speed, time, distance)
   Lesson 16 Historical—water clocks, sand clocks, sun-dials, etc.
         17 Geographical—day, night, sun, moon, seasons, International Date Line.
         18 The story of the calendar.
         19 Nautical measures—knots, ships' logs, speed trial tests, torpedoes.
         20 Domestic science—cooking times (altitudes, cooking on expeditions—Everest) pressure cooking, etc.

APPARATUS:

   Time tables: bus, railway, airline, road, steamship; Continental holiday brochures, Guinness Book of Records, stop watches, reference books in school library, atlases, cookery books, watches, clock, calendar.

CHAPTER FOUR

Types of Lessons

Lessons can be classified according to their purpose and according to the intentions of the teacher. For the student going out on his first school practice it would be profitable to revise what he has been taught about these. Information on the classification of lessons into types can be obtained from several good method books. For ready reference the significant points are listed below.

Four main types of lessons are:

1. *The Development Lesson*—the lesson that develops new learning, making use of the previous knowledge of the children.

2. *The Practice or Skill Lesson*—in which the pupils learn new skills or practice acquired skills.

3. *The Reviewing Lesson*—the lesson in which previous learning is re-appraised, synthesised, recapitulated or reviewed.

4. *The Appreciation Lesson*—the lesson designed mainly to evoke a worth-while emotional or aesthetic reaction.

The Development Lesson

(a) Any new knowledge should, as far as possible, develop out of the previous knowledge and experience of the child. We should proceed from the known to the unknown, or from the familiar to the unfamiliar.

(b) The material should be organised in such a logical sequence that the child is able to see its development, and the common theme that gives it unity.

(c) The lesson should contain new facts coherent to the child, and should add to and illuminate his existing store of knowledge.

(d) In preparing this type of lesson, thought should be given by the student to the way in which new material can be linked to the old, and how interest in the new material can be aroused.

(e) The most common methods employed in Development Lessons are those which make use of narration, questioning, explanation, etc. The student should provide opportunities for activity and participation at all stages of the lesson. There are many things that the children can find out or deduce for themselves.

The Practice or Skill Lesson

Many useful skills in the classroom must be practised until they become routine habits. There are many factors to take into account in this type of lesson:

(a) The meaning of the skill to be acquired should be understood, and its value accepted, by the children.

(b) Long-range goals are not easily understood by the children. The practice or skill to be acquired should be organised in such a way that the achievement of intermediate goals provides the incentives for the child, to sustain his effort and interest.

(c) The student should consider whether the skill to be learned should be taught as a whole or in parts.

(*d*) Drill or practice should come soon after the demonstration of the skill has been given.

(*e*) Distributed practice is better than massed practice, e.g. ten minutes' reading every day is better than fifty minutes' reading on Friday afternoon.

(*f*) The child should be helped to see the usefulness of the skill he is learning by being given opportunities to apply it.

(*g*) The student should be certain that the children are physically and mentally mature enough to benefit from the skill to be taught.

The Reviewing Lesson

The Reviewing Lesson is designed to re-organise and present a different view and clearer understanding of previous learning. In school practice it is most likely to prove useful at the end of the practice, when the student may wish to bring into focus central themes or meanings in the instruction he has given. Techniques which can be used in the Reviewing Lesson are:

(*a*) narration
(*b*) questioning
(*c*) topical outlines
(*d*) blackboard summaries
(*e*) tests, questionnaires, quizzes, etc.
(*f*) visual aids, films, etc.
(*g*) excursions, e.g. in social studies
(*h*) assignments
(*i*) performance, e.g. music, drama, P.E., etc.

The student should be careful that in the more informal of these activities the environment is so manipulated that the important learning is reviewed.

The Appreciation Lesson

Aesthetic appreciation is an emotional reaction as well as an intellectual exercise. Generally speaking, the aim of an Appreciation Lesson will be to foster in the children a receptive attitude towards beauty and to cultivate a sense of discrimination. The following hints are worth considering:

(a) 'Feelings are caught not taught.' 'Unless the teacher himself has the attitude he desires to foster, it is unlikely that he will succeed in communicating it to his pupils.'*

(b) Enjoyment is at the centre of appreciation. Every Appreciation Lesson should prove an enjoyable experience.

(c) Readiness. The student should take care that the emotional response he wishes his pupils to make is not beyond their level of maturity and understanding.

(d) The student's personality should not intrude between the work of art to be appreciated and the pupils. The work of art should hold the centre of the stage.

(e) Creative art is its own justification. Analysis and dissection is often unnecessary and frequently overdone.

Examples of these various types of lessons, and how they may be written up in the lesson note form recommended, can be found in Chapter Five.

* R. A. Oliver *Effective Teaching* (Dent) p. 117.

Preparation—Lesson Notes

The Need for Lesson Notes

Students in colleges of education are required to make some form of lesson notes before they begin to teach a class. The form that these notes take varies from college to college. For example, some colleges make a distinction between fully prepared and outline lesson notes. All, however, insist on some form of written preparation. Why?

(a) Because, in the first place, the student cannot possibly retain everything he is going to teach in his head. He needs some form of reminder of what he is going to teach and how he intends to teach it. The student entering the classroom inadequately prepared might very well be inviting disaster. 'Although every lesson must allow room for free development it must at the same time be organised and have a plan. For this reason lesson notes are not only desirable, but essential.'*

(b) The actual form or layout of the lesson notes makes it necessary for the student to consider factors which he might otherwise ignore or skimp.

(c) The form of lesson notes encourages logical development and preparation.

(d) Lesson notes help to make a student more confident in front of a class.

* H. C. Barnard *An Introduction to Teaching* (U.L.P.) p. 80.

(*e*) Lesson notes direct the attention of the student to *methods* of teaching, i.e. to the *how* of teaching. Merely to be well-versed in a particular subject is certainly not enough to ensure sound learning on the part of the children. The real task of the teacher is knowing how to organise the various classroom activities and learning situations so that the children's understandings are maximised. 'To knowledge of his subject the beginner must ally a knowledge of the successful methods employed in teaching; and, when preparing his lesson, give equal consideration to subject-matter, the "what" of the lesson, and to the method wherein he decides how to teach his subject.'*

(*f*) Lesson notes enable the tutor to anticipate potential difficulties and problems which the inexperienced student might not be able to foresee. The clearer the lesson notes, the more likely it is that valuable advice can be offered in advance of the actual lesson.

(*g*) Lesson notes enable the student's supervisor to provide practical and concrete advice on what the student is attempting to do.

(*h*) Lesson notes enable both the student and the supervisor to assess during and after the lesson whether the student has realised his aim.

How to Use Lesson Notes

'The value of a lesson plan lies not in the final product in the student's note-book, but in the thought and consideration which is given to it.'†

* W. T. Davies and T. B. Shepherd *Teaching: Begin Here* (Epworth Press) p. 29.　　　　　† ibid. p. 35.

Lesson notes should help the student to do his job better than he could do it without them. This does not mean to say that the student should use his lesson notes as a text book, and read them before the class. He should have them available for reference.

Before the lesson begins, if possible, the student should glance through his lesson notes. If they are adequately prepared they should tell him all he needs to know almost at a glance. Furthermore, they will remind him of the equipment, materials, etc. he needs to prepare for the class before the lesson begins. There will be opportunities throughout the lesson when the student can unobtrusively refer to his lesson notes as the different parts of the lesson are reached. The lesson notes will also contain blackboard diagrams, examples, illustrations, etc. which may need to be copied on to the blackboard before the lesson begins.

Lesson notes are not 'strait-jackets'. A well-prepared and sensibly used lesson note plan will normally allow room for manoeuvre. The capacity to exploit the opportunity of the moment is a mature technique and skill, usually born of experience. In most cases, if the student has given due thought and care to the preparation of his lesson notes he will be well advised to keep to his plan of action. The student who makes a habit of deviating from his prepared scheme usually indicates to his tutors that he has not given sufficient and adequate thought to the factors to be borne in mind before preparing a lesson (see Chapter Three).

Having completed the lesson the student has not finished with his lesson notes. Each lesson note and each lesson completed should be a step towards maturity in teaching ability. Most lesson note outlines allow a student to evaluate his success in achieving his aim. More will be said about this in a later chapter. Good lessons can be used again, and can be retained as a basis for modification and improvement. Unsuccessful lessons should not be forgotten. If the student makes this use of his notes he will learn why some lessons were successful and others not.

The Basic Plan and Preamble

Most colleges of education lay down a basic plan of lesson notes which students are expected to follow. These plans vary from college to college, but it might be said that these variations are usually in 'form' rather than in intention. The principles underlying the plans are fundamentally similar. All plans of lesson notes include a Preamble —an account of essential information concerning the lesson. This Preamble will normally contain:

Subject	Date
Class (average age, stream)	Number of children
Aim	Length of lesson
Apparatus	

The remainder of the lesson note plan may vary from college to college. The plan which we consider to be the most versatile and easily understood classifies the body of the lesson under three main headings (i.e. Introduction, Development and Continuation), and separates subject-matter from method.

This form of lesson notes can be used equally well with each type of lesson. The dichotomy between matter and method we consider essential in the preparation stage because it draws attention to the problem of knowing how to teach in addition to knowing what to teach.

There may be no distinction in the children's minds between matter and method. Nevertheless, to deny the existence of both, in formal education, is naïve and evasive. If successful and meaningful learning is to take place, it is essential that the teacher really should differentiate in his own mind between what he is going to teach and how he is going to teach it.

In respect of the subject-matter, C. M. Fleming in *Teaching: A Psychological Analysis* (Methuen, p. 154) recommends the following slogans:

(a) analyse it.
(b) organise it.

'Discover its content. Observe the relationships of its difficulties; and present it in a setting in which insight is invited and understanding becomes possible.'

Teaching efficiency is hampered when not enough thought is given to the problems involved in analysing and organising the work experiences planned for the children.

With this aim in view, we recommend that each of the three sections in the body of the lesson be divided into further sub-sections with Matter or Content on the left-hand side of the page, and Method on the right-hand side.

Thus the body of the lesson notes containing the Introduction, Development and Continuation will be arranged as shown on the next page:

39

Matter	Method
Introduction	
Development	
Continuation	

The Introduction

The Introduction to the lesson should do one or more of the following things:

(*a*) create a desire in the pupils to participate in the lesson.

(*b*) create an atmosphere conducive to the attainment of the aim of the lesson. This would be particularly relevant in lessons with an emotional or aesthetic aim.

(*c*) recall previous knowledge. The Introduction may provide a 'link' between the 'known' and the 'unknown'. In many Development lessons we may consider that the knowledge already possessed by the children will serve as a 'host' for new knowledge (see N. Catty *A First Book on Teaching* (Methuen)). The revision of the previously learned knowledge may produce the feeling of a need for new or additional learning.

(*d*) arouse interest. This in a sense will be true of all introductions whatever the aim of the lesson may be.

(*e*) produce a smooth transition. The Introduction

might involve a change of direction from the lesson in which the children have been previously engaged. There may be a change of emotion, e.g. a transition from a games lesson to a singing lesson.

(f) state a purpose or present a problem for which a solution is sought. It is important that the child should also appreciate the purpose of the lesson.

Introduction—Matter

In this section the student should state clearly and concisely *what* he is going to do. For example, in a Science lesson for ten-year olds on 'Water—A Vital Need', the Introduction (Matter) might establish a general body of knowledge which the children already have about water and its uses. Or, again, the Introduction (Matter) of the lesson might be a challenging question to stimulate discussion of the topic.

Introduction—Method

Here the student will state *how* he intends to establish what is known about water, or how he intends to use the challenging question as an introduction.

A word of advice. It is important here to emphasise the need for careful, precise and detailed preparation of this part of the lesson notes. In this section the student's lesson notes often contain many meaningless and totally irrelevant remarks, which do not indicate how he intends to teach. Remarks such as 'to stimulate the children's interest in water' do not explain the *means* whereby the student is going to do this. Another well-worn phrase is 'Ask the children questions'. This is not much better than the previous statement because the interest aroused will depend upon the phrasing, meaningfulness and particular relevance of the questions used. Many questions asked are ambiguous. The art of questioning is not easy. It needs to be practised and, for the student, questions need careful thought and working out (see Chapter Eight). The sound Introduction—Method section will contain some examples of the questions to be asked. Most certainly the first few questions should be included, and possibly a framework of subsequent questions which will make clear the student's intentions.

Development—Matter

This section of the lesson notes should contain the *core* of the lesson. The new material of learning will grow out of the Introduction and add to the child's previous experience and understanding. Thus it will have meaning and coherence for the child, being a logical development of the Introduction. Normally, as a result of careful analysis and organisation of the subject-matter, the Development will proceed by logical stages or sequences which should be clearly apparent in the student's lesson notes. For example, in the lesson on 'Water—A Vital Need':

Development: Stage 1. Water as a food which all living things need.

Stage 2. Water in the foods we eat.

Stage 3. Streams—above and below ground.

Stage 4. Our drinking water—wells and reservoirs.

A common fault of many lessons, at this stage, is that of presenting too many facts which are often isolated and unrelated. D. E. M. Gardner writes of the danger of presenting great quantities of facts for the children to 'goggle at' rather than to utilise. Children should be aware of the continuity of the material and should be able to see the common thread or main theme which gives it unity.

Development—Method

As each stage in the Development is written down, the student should indicate how he proposes to develop the point. Remarks in the Method section (e.g. 'Tell the story', 'draw a map', or 'write examples') are inadequate. In the case of 'telling the story' the student should draw up an outline of the main points in the story. If this is to be punctuated with questions, the main types of questions to be asked are needed. If the blackboard is going to be used then, again, the lesson notes should show the purpose of this. In mathematics lessons, for instance, the examples to be used in the lesson should be prepared and tested beforehand and included in the notes. Maps, pictorial illustrations and diagrams should be recorded under the Development—Method section at the appropriate stage of the Development.

It might be said, at this point, that children need time to savour and assimilate learning. To try to present too much—too many facts in too little time—in the Development stage of the lesson usually serves to confuse the children. It is very difficult to gauge in advance a time-schedule for the completion of each stage of the lesson, but the student should remember that a lesson must have balance, i.e. a balance of its three parts—beginning, middle and end. The exigencies of the situation will determine the proportions of that balance. What should be avoided, however, is the situation where the lesson ends and the student finds himself half-way through the Development section, with the matter undeveloped and the continuity and unity of the lesson destroyed.

The Continuation

In the last stage of the lesson note writing, the word 'Continuation' has been used deliberately in preference to such terms as 'Summary', 'Children's Work', 'Conclusion', 'Recapitulation', 'Application', 'Class Activity', 'Class Participation', etc.

Continuation is preferable to Class Activity, Class Participation or Application, because the student may imagine that 'activity' or 'children's work' is confined to the end of the lesson when, in fact, there should be *activity* throughout the lesson. Continuation is preferable to Summary or Recapitulation because not all lessons lend themselves to immediate revision or summary by the teacher or by the pupils. Learning takes time, and children need to be allowed time to think about what has been taught. Thus the summary or recapitulation can sometimes be a disruption of this process of assimilation. Most lessons, moreover, are not ends in themselves but rather parts of a general scheme or comprehensive aim.

Continuation—Matter

This section might be used for any of the following purposes:

(a) to prepare for subsequent lessons on a similar theme.

(*b*) to summarise the new learning.

(*c*) to recapitulate the new learning taught during the lesson.

(*d*) to synthesise or reconstruct isolated points or facts which have emerged in the lesson.

(*e*) to revise.

(*f*) to give further practice—this is particularly necessary in a skill-forming lesson where a skill might recently have been taught.

(*g*) application—in all lessons opportunities should be provided for the children to use new skills and new learning.

(*h*) to review, in the sense of giving a new look to familiar learning, or directing the attention of the class to subject-matter that has been given a different focus.

(*i*) to initiate activity; this does not mean that activity does not take place at other stages in the lesson.

(*j*) to evaluate the learning that has taken place through testing or questioning.

Continuation—Method

Some methods that can be employed in the Continuation section are:

(*a*) *Blackboard summary*. The student should state whether this is to be pre-arranged, or built up as the lesson develops. If the first method is used, reference should be made to this in the lesson notes.

(*b*) *Writing notes*. Students should state whether they are to be done independently by the children or with guidance. If with guidance—what guidance?

(c) *Illustration.* Students should give examples of the choice of subjects to be illustrated.

(d) *Exercises.* If these are to be taken from a text book, the page number and title of the book should be included. If the student compiles his own exercises they should be carefully prepared and recorded in the lesson notes.

(e) *Model-making.* The student should give details of the material to be used, etc.

(f) *Dramatisation.* This needs great care in preparation. Thought should be given to the number of participants, how non-participants are to be occupied, re-arrangement of the room, etc.

(g) *Oral questioning.* The types of questions to be used, or the general framework of the questions, should be recorded.

(h) *Tests or quizzes.* The student should give an account of the test he proposes to set or the method to be employed in the quiz.

(i) *Assignments.* Full details should be recorded.

(j) *Group research.* The size of the groups, organisation, names of the children in the groups, and details of the sources to be used should be given.

(k) *Project.* Any simplified project to be used as a continuation of an ordinary lesson should have the details noted.

(l) *Group discussion.* Though the outcome of this may be unpredictable, the method of organising it should be clearly stated.

(m) *Individual, group, class-controlled or free activity.* This also needs careful organisation and recording.

Specimen Lesson Notes

Example A: Development Lesson

SUBJECT: Geography

CLASS: Fourth year (average age 11½)

DATE:

NUMBER: 40 (mixed)

DURATION: 60 mins.

AIM: To teach the children the principal methods used in sea fishing, i.e. Trawling, Drifting. (This is the specific aim of a lesson embodied in a scheme of work entitled 'Where we get our Food').

APPARATUS: Wall map (White Fish Authority). Pictures of Trawlers and Drifters. 40 copies—Philips Pictorial Atlas. Materials provided by children.

Cartridge paper. Black sticky paper. Crayons. 20 pairs scissors.

MATTER	METHOD
Introduction Arousing interest in the subject of fishing.	The pupils' attention is drawn to the large map supplied by the White Fish Authority, and to the pictures of fishing drifters and trawlers displayed on the classroom walls for several days. The pupils have been asked, in a previous lesson, to find out all they can about different kinds of sea fish round our shores, from their local fish shop, newspapers, magazines, books and encyclopaedias, etc.

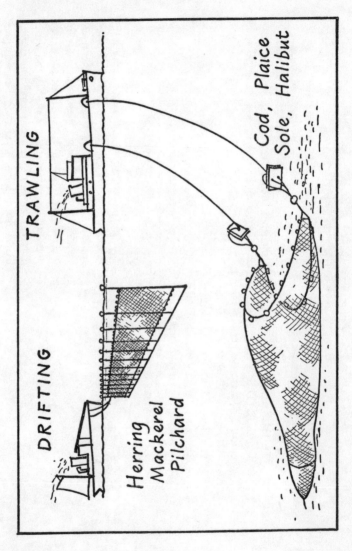

MATTER	METHOD
	Individual children will be invited to show the class any pictures, or retail any information, they have obtained.
Development	
Stage 1	
Two main methods of catching fish:	Teacher's narrative account. Details added to blackboard diagram as lesson proceeds (see illustration). Obtain information on how method operates by questioning, e.g.
(i) Trawlers and Trawling.	
Type of boat.	
Size 80–200 ft.	Why is net weighted?
Bag type nets or trawls.	Why are floats used?
Floats, bobbins, otter boards, cod end, winching gear, etc.	What is the purpose of otter boards?
	Why do you think the net is called a trawl?
	Diagram of trawler and trawl.
Stage 2	Narrative account. Details elicited by questioning and added to blackboard diagram as lesson develops, e.g.
(ii) Drifters and Drifting.	
Size of boat.	
Method of catching.	Why do you think this type of boat is called a drifter?
Floats, buoys, messenger rope, nets, etc.	In what way is the method used different from that of the trawler?
	What is the difference between the buoy and the float?
	Diagram of drifter and drifting.

MATTER

Stage 3

Different kinds of fish: plaice, halibut, sole, herring, pilchard, mackerel, cod. Different shapes. Different habitats. Different methods necessary in order to catch them.

METHOD

By questioning. Examine all the different pictures of fish brought in by children. Make a blackboard list of names of fish. Underline most important species. Through questioning separate those fish caught by trawlers from those caught by drifters, e.g.

  What shape is a plaice?
  Why do you think it is flat?
  How do you think it will be caught?
  Cod are not flat, but they are caught by trawlers—why?

  Draw up blackboard summary as answers are given.

Blackboard Summary

FISH	WHERE FOUND	HOW CAUGHT
Plaice	sea bed	trawl
Sole	sea bed	trawl
Halibut	sea bed	trawl

Herring	surface	drifter
Mackerel	surface	drifter
Pilchard	surface	drifter
Cod	sea bed	trawl

Written summary on blackboard:
'Trawlers catch fish that live and swim near the bottom of the sea.'
'Drifters catch fish that live and swim near the surface of the sea.'

MATTER	METHOD
Continuation Group Assignments: 1. Map of main fishing ports. 2. Map of fishing grounds used by British ships and fish found there. 3. Cross-section diagram of trawler. 4. Cross-section diagram of drifter. 5. Wall diagram showing appropriate fish being caught by trawler and drifter.	Children arranged in groups—free choice. Choice will be influenced by materials produced by individuals. Group leaders appointed. Whole scheme explained to class in outline. Group assignments explained separately to groups. Completed assignments displayed on wall—see illustration. Illustration showing layout of wall display (see illustration on next page).

MAP
showing the main fishing ports and the tonnage

CROSS SECTION DIAGRAM
of a drifter

MONTAGE PICTURE
showing trawlers and drifters with various types of fish at appropriate depths

MAP
showing sea areas in which various types of fish are caught

CROSS SECTION DIAGRAM
of a trawler

DISPLAY TABLE
for relevant literature, models, specimens, collections, etc.

Example B: Appreciation Lesson

SUBJECT:	Art	DATE:
CLASS:	Fourth year (average age 11+)	NUMBER: 40 (mixed)
		DURATION: 55 mins.

AIM: To stimulate the creative imagination of the children, by helping them to enjoy the nonsense poem 'The Pobble That Had No Toes' by Edward Lear. (The children have read several nonsense poems by Lear, Gilbert, Carroll and others in their poetry lessons.)

APPARATUS: Two pieces of cartridge paper.
Paints.
Brushes.
Pencils.
Water pots.
Newspaper.
Palettes.
Copy of the poem 'The Pobble That Had No Toes'.

MATTER	METHOD
Introduction	
The poem.	Reading by the teacher without comment.
Development	
Stage 1	
Arousing interest. Encouraging use of imagination.	Questioning by the teacher. What does the Pobble look like? Would you like to hear the poem again?

MATTER

Stage 2
Second reading.

Stage 3
Closer investigation of poet's intention.

Stage 4
Thinking and using imagination.

Continuation
Application of ideas in illustration.

METHOD

Reading by the teacher—accentuating descriptive sections but no further comment.

Questioning.
Ask for several interpretations from the children. What does the poet actually tell us? 1. No toes. 2. Nose wrapped in flannel. What does it look like? Does it look like you or me? etc. How many legs has the Pobble?

Children close eyes. Think about Pobbles. What do you see? Children are asked to the blackboard to sketch their idea. Comment and discussion. Who else thinks it has a beak? What else could it have? i.e. a mouth, a trunk, a snout, etc.

Children are asked to paint their impression of what *they* think the Pobble looks like. They can paint several views of it from different angles. No two ideas should be exactly alike. If time permits, the children can illustrate how they think the Pobble lost its toes.

Example C: Development Lesson

SUBJECT:	Oral Composition
CLASS:	Third year (average age 10½)
	DATE:
	NUMBER: 40 (boys)
	DURATION: 30 mins.

AIM: To stimulate an interest in writing and to give the children opportunity and practice in studying and discussing magazines—as an introductory lesson to starting a wall magazine.

MATTER	METHOD
Introduction Children study magazines in order to observe the variety of types of contributions they contain.	Teacher asks children to look at the magazines which they were asked to bring to the lesson. All children should have at least one magazine. (Magazines may be for adults or children, parish magazines, specialist magazines, etc.)
Development *Stage 1* Classification of contents into wide main groups.	Teacher points out that most people buy magazines for their variety of content. Nearly all magazines contain a large variety of articles. What sort of things are printed in the magazines you have brought? Teacher draws up a blackboard list.

MATTER

METHOD

Magazines usually have:
News   Features on:
Stories   Sport
Serials   Pets
Pictures   Hobbies
Puzzles   Geography
Jokes   History
Cartoons   Local Interest
Strip Cartoons Nature Study, etc.
Crosswords
Competitions
Advertisements

Stage 2
Discovering and investigating magazines in closer detail.

Teacher questions class. How many children have magazines with features in? Number written on blackboard in appropriate place. Continues down list.

Stage 3
Further scrutiny to produce knowledge that certain items deserve greater space allocation.

Teacher questions the class. Which items on the list take up most space in your magazine? Which is most important, etc.?

Continuation
Introducing wall magazine for class.
Deciding space allocation.

Teacher (*a*) explains that he intends to produce a wall magazine for the classroom.
(*b*) Deciding space allocation. How many people will be needed to contribute the various items? (Discourage excessive contributions of jokes, puzzles, crosswords, cartoons, etc.)
(*c*) Teacher explains that in the next lesson various officials will be appointed. There will be:

  A chief editor
  A news editor
  A sports editor
  A features editor, etc.
(*d*) Children must think about this in preparation for the next lesson.

Example D: Practice or Skill Lesson

SUBJECT: Mathematics
CLASS: Third year (average age 9)

DATE:
NUMBER: 20 (mixed)
DURATION: 45 mins.

AIM: To give the children practice in weighing, and to improve their concept of weight by exercises in estimation.

APPARATUS: 2 sets of scales.
Sand, clay, marbles, dried peas, jam jars, powder paint tins, and assorted containers.
Set of weights.
Prepared bags 100g, 200g, 400g, 500g, 1kg, 1·5kg.

MATTER	METHOD
Introduction	
Estimating game using sets of 6 different pre-pared weights. (This is a revision game used in a previous lesson, and an introduction and preparation for the Development.)	Children are told that bags have been weighed. They are either 100-g, 200-g, 400-g, 500-g, 1-kg or 1·5-kg bags. Each bag is numbered. Bags are passed round the class. Children estimate and record weight and number of bag. Teacher reads out the answers.

Development
Estimating weights of various materials. Calculating by subtraction the error of estimation.

Stage 1
Plan for recording details prepared on the blackboard, e.g.

TIN OF:	ESTIMATED WEIGHT	ACTUAL WEIGHT	DIFFERENCE
Peas			
Sand			
Clay			
Marbles			

MATTER

METHOD

Stage 2
Teacher fills tin with peas. Writes his estimate of weight.
Stage 3
Teacher weighs tin. Children watch. Teacher writes the actual weight.

MATTER

METHOD

Stage 4
Teacher calculates the difference as a demonstration subtraction sum on the blackboard.

Stage 5
Process repeated with sand, clay and marbles. Individual children assisting and calculating. Remainder of class watching.

Continuation
Children's activity. Repeating the processes demonstrated by the teacher, working in pairs, using the same materials but different containers.

Same as before—except working in pairs, and children recording results in plan written in their exercise books.

Near end of lesson, 4 or more completed records of differences are added together to see which pair of children have won the game of accurate estimation.

Example E: Reviewing Lesson

SUBJECT: History

CLASS: 4A (average age 14)

DATE:

NUMBER: 35 (boys)

DURATION: 45 mins.

GENERAL AIM: To examine and consider the social and economic conditions which brought about the development of means of transport in the 18th century.

SPECIFIC AIM: By means of review, to show that industrial development on a large scale would have been impossible if means of transport had not been improved. (Class have had a series of lessons on the Industrial Revolution, the rise of industry, new inventions and the growth of factory towns, the increase in manufactured goods, population rise, etc.)

MATTER	METHOD
Introduction Revising the history of the early period of the Industrial Revolution.	By narration and questioning. (The teacher aims to show the class that before and during the early period of the Industrial Revolution the existing means of transport sufficed for the economy of the country.) What were the early factories like in size? What were the usual methods of ownership of them? Where were these factories usually located? Why?

MATTER	METHOD
	What other factors affected the location of factories?
	What were the disadvantages of water as a means of power?
	Teacher sums up so far—Industry at first appears to have been scattered along the rivers. Development of industry was limited by the uncertainty of water power and the slowness of water transport.
Development *Stage 1* Reasons why large-scale industry was impossible during this time. Examination of existing methods of transport—rivers. Disadvantages of river transport.	By questioning and blackboard use. River transport is cheap, but what were the defects of rivers as means of transport?
Stage 2 Examination of existing methods of transport—roads.	By questioning. What were the roads like in England before the Industrial Revolution? Were there any 'made' roads? Why had road-making been neglected in England?

Stage 3
Summary of Stages 1 and 2.

Teacher reads extracts (writings of Arthur Young) emphasising the urgent transport problem in the early 18th century. Blackboard summary.

An urgent transport problem because of:
(*a*) the growth of internal trade
(*b*) the expansion of industry
(*c*) the inadequate state of existing means of transport.

Stage 4
Efforts made to solve transport problems—building of roads. The turnpike roads. Road-builders: Telford, Macadam, Metcalf. Construction of canals. Advantages of the new canals over the roads. Effects on trade and development of ports.

By narration and questioning:
Why did not the Government set about improving roads during the early part of the 18th century?
In what ways, initially, were the roads improved?
Who were the famous road-builders?
How did their methods differ?
What were the particular advantages of building canals?
What advantages did canals have over roads?

MATTER	METHOD
Continuation	
Stages in the Industrial Revolution and comparable transport development.	Class to make their own outline summary of the lesson by filling in the framework of the summary written on the blackboard by the teacher.

Enlarge this outline with your own notes:

There was an urgent transport problem in the 18th century because of the inadequacy of existing means of transport.

The roads.

Early efforts to improve the roads.

The work of the great road builders.

The economic effects of road improvement.

The improvement of river transport.

The advantages of the canals.

The economic effects of building canals.

General effects of transport improvement in Britain.

Alternative Plans

From his general reading of educational method books the student will be aware that there is a variety of ideas on how to write up lesson notes. Furthermore, the terminology of the stages in lesson note preparation varies from book to book. It may be that the reader has been recommended to use a plan different from the one we have outlined. Because so many of these alternatives exist we have listed a few of the most representative of them.

First Plan. Based on *Effective Teaching* by R. A. Oliver (Dent (Canada) Ltd.).

Usual stages in teaching a lesson:

1. An introductory step.
2. A statement of the purpose of the lesson or of a problem for which a solution is sought.
3. The presentation of the subject matter.
4. The application of the results achieved.

These stages can be summarised in title form:

1. Introduction
2. Aim (or Problem)
3. Presentation
4. Application (or Expression)

In one of Oliver's plans he recommends that subject-matter and method should be separated. The Presentation section of the lesson plan should be divided by a line drawn vertically down the page. Thus the lesson outline based on this plan would appear as follows:

Subject:
Lesson Topic:
Class:
Pupils' Aims:
Student Teacher's Aims:

---

1. *Introduction.*
2. *Problem* (or other statement of lesson's purpose).
3. *Presentation.*

Matter or Content	*Method or Procedure*
(Outline of what is to be taught.)	(Outline of how the student intends to teach.)

4. *Application or Expression.*

Second Plan. Based on *Teaching: Begin Here* by W. T. Davies and T. B. Shepherd (Epworth Press).

Stages in teaching a lesson:

1. *Aim.*
2. *Introduction:* (a) arousing interest
   (b) providing continuity
   (c) preparing the class.
3. *Development:* (a) presenting new information
   (b) revision
   (c) summary.
4. *Conclusion:* (a) general revision
   (b) application and testing.

Davies and Shepherd, while appreciating the value of separating matter from method, claim that it is not always convenient to do this in a notebook. In the plans provided by them in their book they emphasise method rather than the subject-matter to be taught, for they assume that every student will know his facts thoroughly before he begins to teach.

Third Plan. Based on *Principles of Teaching* by W. M. Ryburn (Oxford).

Steps in lessons:

1. *Preparation:* (*a*) previous knowledge of children
                  (*b*) arousing interest.
2. *Statement of Aim* (so that the pupils know exactly what they are to do and where they are going).
3. *Introduction.*
4. *Development.*
5. *Formulation.* (*Generalisation.*)
6. *Application.*

Ryburn suggests that the layout should be varied according to the type of lesson being prepared. He discusses three types of lessons in his book, viz. the lesson for the acquisition of knowledge; the lesson for the acquisition of skill; and the lesson for the development of appreciation. The lesson plans for each type are:

Acquisition of Knowledge

1. *Preparation and Aim.*
2. *Introduction.*
3. *Development.*
4. *Formulation* (or *Generalisation*).
5. *Application.*

Acquirement of Skills

  1. *Preparation and Aim.*
  2. *Development.*
  3. *Practice and Corrections.*
  4. *Revision.*

Appreciation of the Arts

  1. *Preparation and Aim.*
  2. *Presentation.*
  3. *Discussion.*
  4. *Practice.*

Fourth Plan. Based on *The Principles of Teaching Method* by A. Pinsent (Harrap).

Pinsent lists the practical steps to be taken in organising a 'unit of work' as follows:

  1. *Introduction:* (*a*) organisation of mental set
                 (*b*) statement of aim.

  2. *Main Body of Unit:* (*a*) presentation
                 (*b*) guidance—(i) Analysis
                        (ii) Abstraction
                        (iii) Synthesis.

  3. *A Rounding-off Section:*
        (*a*) recapitulation
        (*b*) permanent record
        (*c*) follow-up, diagnosis and remedy
        (*d*) application—practice and exercise.

For a specific Development Lesson, Pinsent recommends the headings:

1. *Introduction.*
2. *Presentation.*
3. *Practice.*
4. *Application.*

For a specific Appreciation Lesson, Pinsent recommends:

1. *Preparation of pupils.*
2. *Presentation.*
3. *Guidance.*
4. *Creation.*

Fifth Plan. Based on *A First Book on Teaching* by N. Catty (Methuen).

The most distinctive feature of Catty's suggestions is that the subject-matter and subject-method should be divided into two columns, the *teacher's work* and the *children's work*. Thus a typical lesson outline plan would appear as follows:

Class: *Subject:*
Time: *Apparatus:*
Aim:
Previous Knowledge:

Teacher's Work	Children's Work
Introduction.	
Development:	
1.	
2.	
3., etc.	
Application.	

Sixth Plan. Based on *Learning and Teaching* by Hughes and Hughes (Longmans).

Hughes and Hughes recommend that the underlying distinction between Matter and Method should be borne in mind but that these should *not* be separated in notes by a line drawn down the middle of the page.

They also recommend that the five stages known as the Herbartian Steps in learning should be carefully considered, i.e. preparation, presentation, association, generalisation and application.

Without recommending a formalised plan for any type of lesson, they suggest that every lesson should contain the following stages:

1. *Beginning.*
2. *Development:* (*a*) exposition or demonstration
    (*b*) individual work by pupils.
3. *Conclusion.*

The striking thing about these alternatives listed is that they have a unanimity of purpose despite the use they make of different phraseology. They are all suggestions aimed at providing the student with a framework which will enable him to give effective lessons. There are general principles inherent in teaching, and all these alternative methods are consistent in their recognition of them.

The whole purpose of writing lesson notes can be understood as a preliminary exercise or discipline designed for the apprentice-teacher, which will allow modification and adaptation as skill, technique, ability and confidence develop.

'The young teacher cannot be too earnestly warned that for him the great thing is to appropriate the "spirit" of the formal steps of the teaching process without becoming enslaved to their "letter". And how much does this mean? It means that, though all the steps are not necessarily gone through in the treatment of any one section or unit of teaching, yet the order in which the steps occur cannot be departed from without disadvantage. That the acquisition of knowledge or of skill is a process of assimilation of new to old, that the relevant parts of the pupils' previously acquired stock of ideas should therefore be recalled first, that there should be a progress from the concrete and particular to the abstract or general, that ideas must be possessed before they can be applied, and that application in its turn makes for effective and permanent possession: these are truths as sure as the law of gravitation because they embody the plain facts of the working of a child's mind. . . . Like the rules of any other art, however, the rules of the teaching art will not always be overtly employed. As soon as the teacher has thoroughly imbibed their spirit he may be left quite free to dispense with a formal array of preparation, presentation and the rest. But though the steps may no longer be explicitly stated, or even thought of, they will always remain implicit in his best efforts, and he will be wise enough not to despise them because he has learnt to practise his art without conscious need of their help.'*

* T. Raymont *The Principles of Education* (Longmans).

CHAPTER SIX

Modified Teaching Plans, Units of Work and Projects

It has already been stressed that there is no one way of recording lesson notes and that the main purpose of preparation is to help the student to deal adequately with the teaching situations he encounters.

In this chapter we shall consider a number of variations on the suggestions already made. These will include:

1. Modification of lesson note recording for more experienced students.

2. Modification of lesson note recording for some specialist subjects, e.g. Woodwork, Metalwork, Physical Education, Domestic Science, etc.

3. Modified preparation for planning units of work.

4. Preparing projects.

Modified Lesson Notes for More Experienced Students

Previous chapters have been concerned with advice to students starting their training. The teaching situation on the final school practice should more closely resemble that experienced by the qualified teacher. The student will have developed in teaching maturity—his initial apprenticeship is coming to an end. It follows that the detailed lesson note writing necessary in the earlier stages of training should be developing into that kind of preparation which is more characteristic of the experienced teacher.

When on final school practice, students are often required to teach a full time-table, and the increasing demands on their time make the elaborate writing-up of every single lesson both impracticable and unrealistic. There is a need to concentrate on essentials and use time to the best advantage. Reduction in the amount of preparation is undesirable—but methods of planning and recording can be condensed. In fact, one mark of the student's increasing competence will be his ability to free himself from the need to record in great detail.

In the final year, preparation for school practice should be more scheme-oriented and less concerned with the preparation of separate lessons. The student is more able to appreciate the importance of continuity and related learning experiences and therefore must plan in relation to the scheme as a whole. This suggests that greater time and care should be given to the development of the scheme of work, thus permitting a reduction in the amount of lesson recording. As the preparation of the scheme expands, the detailed recording of lesson notes is reduced. Nevertheless, effective teaching will necessitate the inclusion of a number of essential details in lesson notes. These will include:

(a) the specific aim of the lesson;

(b) materials needed by the teacher, or by the pupils;

(c) special needs for a particular lesson, e.g. organisation, special equipment, complex planning or explanation. These will vary according to individual requirements.

Finally, modern educational thought emphasises the importance of courses or units of experience rather than set, separate lessons.* The more mature student should give greater consideration to the detailed development of the scheme of work (looking at the scheme of work as a course and planning for the pupils' learning experiences which are part of an organised unit). For example, in a Science scheme of work on 'Heat', detailed planning of the course (as in the example given below) reduces the need to prepare full lesson notes.

Example of a Scheme of Work

SUBJECT: General Science

PARTICULARS OF CHILDREN: Age: 12+
                                       Sex: Mixed
                                       Form: 1B
                                       Number: 30

SUBJECT MATTER:

(*a*) *Lessons*—2 lessons of 60 minutes per week for 3 weeks.

(*b*) *General Aim*—To develop children's concepts of heat and temperature in as many practical ways as possible.

(*c*) *Previous Knowledge*—Assumes little formal instruction in science; the scheme is designed to draw upon previous knowledge from everyday living and to examine this in a scientific way.

* See A. G. & E. H. Hughes *Learning and Teaching* (Longmans), p. 383.

SCHEME OF WORK:

Heat and Temperature

Week 1   Lesson 1   How Man and Animals Keep Warm

Small group work—6 groups of 5, work card direction.
Work card examples:

Man and Clothing—in various regions of the earth.
Man and Housing—insulation, damp courses, houses in different parts of the world.
Animals—skin, fur, hibernation, etc.

Reporting in Groups—Tchr. summary on blackboard; children recording on large tchr.-made summary chart.
Materials—library facilities and school texts.

Week 1   Lesson 2

Experiment—Which type of clothing keeps us warmest? Cotton, wool, nylon.

Equipment—per group—4 tins, pieces of wool, cotton, nylon, thermometers, 1 kettle.

Week 2   Lesson 3   Conductors and Non-conductors

Experiment i. Substances which pass on heat quickly and substances which pass on heat slowly.

Equipment—Candle, 3-inch piece of wire, nail, piece of thin glass rod, piece of pot, clay, brick. Holding different substances in candle flame; recording their heat-conducting qualities.

Experiment ii. Equipment—hot water, tin can, plastic beaker. Put hot water in tin can and in plastic beaker. Which container gets hotter?

Experiment iii. Tchr. demonstrates that water can boil at the top of a container whilst remaining cold at the bottom.

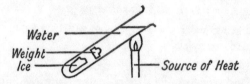

Experiment iv. Tchr. demonstrates, plunging penny on horizontal sheet of paper down into bunsen flame and out again. Pattern of scorch marks examined and discussed.

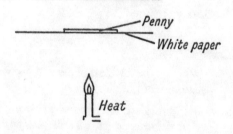

Experiment v. Tchr. demonstrates that water can be boiled in a paper cup over a flame. What happens if the paper cup is empty?

Experiment vi. Heating one end of a horizontal brass bar which has rivets held to it with paraffin wax. (*a*) Observation—rivet fall—wax melting—heat spread. (*b*) Order of rivet fall—way in which heat spreads (conduction).

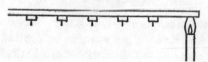

Week 2   Lesson 4

Application of previous lesson. Work cards for groups. Finding out and reporting to class. Example of work cards:

Why do we use table mats?

Why do we wear gloves in winter?

Why can ice-cream be kept solid longer by wrapping it in newspaper?

In addition—Make up 2 questions on 'heat' to pass on to another group. Make a list of good and bad conductors.

Week 3   Lesson 5   Expansion of Metals

Experiment—by one group, rest observe.
To find out what effect heat has on a length of wire.

Equipment—wire, weight, string, candle.

Questions: What happens to wire when heated?
What happens to wire when it cools?
What happens to telegraph wires on a hot day?
What happens to railway lines on a hot day?
Therefore . . .

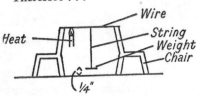

Experiment—Tchr. demonstrates—using bar and gauge and ball and ring experiments to show expansion.

Application—Discussion with class and preparation of topic assignments for next lesson. Sources of information.

Week 3   Lesson 6

Group topics—discuss and report on the problems to do with expansion which face bridge builders, clock and watch makers, railway engineers, manned rocket designers. Use of library facilities and text books, etc.

Five-minute presentations by groups to allow for teacher and class comments and discussion.

Modified Lesson Notes for Specialists

Because of the particular requirements (materials, methods, content, approach, etc.) in specialist subjects, it might be necessary to write these lessons up in different ways.

In the specimen lesson notes for Physical Education which follow on the next page, although the arrangement differs from that outlined in Chapter 5, there is still a clear indication of matter and method, and an obvious sequence of development through the lesson. The points of particular importance in this lesson, i.e. 'What the teacher says' and 'What to look for when coaching', are given a significant part in the overall preparation.

Preparation of Units of Work

Students teaching in Infant Schools, or in a few 'progressive' Junior Schools, will often be required to plan, from the outset, learning experiences made up of units of work rather than separate lessons. Indeed, the day-to-day timetables of such schools are organised for units of work and not divided into separate lesson periods.

In this situation, important points to remember are:

(*a*) this kind of teaching needs wider, more imaginative and more detailed planning. (Continued on page 83.)

Specimen Lesson Notes   Physical Education Lesson

CLASS: IA   AGE: 11–12   TIME OF LESSON: 9.20–10.0 a.m.

NUMBER IN CLASS: 32

APPARATUS (to be used in Part I): 32 small balls
32 individual mats

FRAMEWORK:

APPROX. TIME	ACTIVITY AND WHAT THE TEACHER SAYS	COACHING POINTS
Part I		
Introductory Activity (1–3 mins.)	When you get into the gym take a small ball and practise any throwing and catching activity. Change to running, keeping the ball close to your feet. Stop and control ball on a signal.	Use all the space. Eye on the ball. Move your feet. Bring the ball into the body. Tie the ball to your feet.
Footwork (2–5 mins.)	Put away your ball, take a mat and show me how high you can jump over your mat. Think about your landing too. Now jump off two feet and show a stretch shape. How can you improve your jump? Show me. Repeat your jump and improve it.	Reach for the ceiling. Stretch for the floor. Demonstration to show take-off, height and landing.

APPROX. TIME	ACTIVITY AND WHAT THE TEACHER SAYS	COACHING POINTS
Trunk Movements (2–4 mins.)	Change to rolling forwards and backwards along your mat. Now get on to your feet at the end of each roll. How can you improve the flow? Show me a bridge shape over your mat. Change to another, and then twist to a third. Repeat these, trying to improve the quality.	Reach forward with the hands. Push with hands when going back. Demonstration if appropriate.
Arm and Shoulder (2–4 mins.)	Practise different ways of taking your weight on hands and making hips or feet the highest point—come down as quietly as you can.	Hands shoulder width apart. Point your chin at the floor. Try to hold a balance. Remember hand forward and twist when coming down.
Part II		
Class Activity (4–10 mins.)	*Apparatus*—6 benches, 2 beams (balance side up at No. 3), 6 mats (6 ft. × 4 ft. Recticel), 2 agility mats.	Stress—1. Variety 2. Control. Eliminate queueing.
1st Lesson only. Next 3 or 4 lessons no class activity.	Running and jumping off the benches— something as you land on the mat—use the	Future lessons develop own sequence, then qua-

Additional time on group work.

floor space and wall bar and go back over the bench taking weight on hands.

lity of movements within sequence—flow or continuity.

How can you improve the quality of your landings? Show me.

Can you improve the flow from one movement to another?

Group Work
1st Lesson
(10 mins.)
Subsequent Lessons
(20–25 mins.)

Groups as for class activity.
1. 2 beams at 4 and 14. Inclined bench on 14. 4 individual mats.
2. Horse crosswise, nat (6 × 4), ropes.
3. Bench, mat. Inclined bench on wall bar.
4. As in class activity.
5. As Group I.
6. Buck, mat (6 × 4), ropes.
7. Box crosswise, 2 sections. Mat (6 × 4). Inclined bench.
8. As in class activity.

Tasks:

1 and 5. Pre-positional activities along beam and down bench. Transfer hands to feet, feet to hands, on individual mats.

2 and 6. Cross apparatus in different ways, use wallbars, and return by ropes to halfway.

3 and 7. Crossing apparatus with feet at the highest point.

4 and 8. Development of class activity.

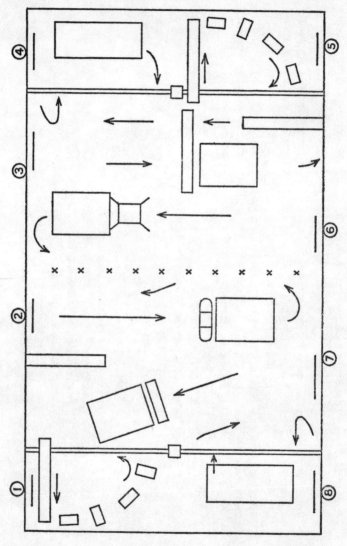

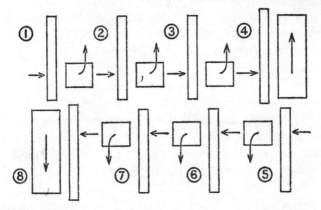

(*b*) greater flexibility is required, and a wide variety of methods (e.g. demonstration, discussion, experiment, reporting, group study, etc.) need to be considered.

(*c*) frequent evaluation by the teacher of what has been achieved is necessary.

Preparing Projects

Students on school practice may be given a project to carry out as part of their work. Clearly, this cannot be prepared in the same way as a more formal and controlled class lesson. A more suitable plan and lay-out would be one which resembles a scheme of work.

The following points should be considered:

(*a*) Preparation—In the initial stages of planning, the student should take an imaginative overall view and explore the possibilities and range of the topic.

The first part of the project work must be designed to present this viewpoint to the children, so that they have more appreciation of the work involved.

The preparation and organisation should be adjusted to fit the individual and group interests of the children. Thus, it is essential that the children's interests should be known.

(b) Materials—The variety of materials required to sustain interest in the project should be readily available.

(c) Subjects included—The project may grow to encompass almost every subject in the curriculum. The student should know which subjects can be included within the scope of the project and how he can best use them.

(d) Organisation—In planning a project, attention should be given to the following points:

What is the teacher's contribution to be?

How will the children be grouped?

How will the finished work be presented? (e.g. display, reporting, models, books, etc.)

How will the work be co-ordinated so that the different parts of the plan are communicated to the whole class?

Which part of the work will be done in groups?

Which part will be done by individuals?

Which part will be done as a class?

(e) Evaluation—Planning should continue throughout the project because modification of the original plans may be necessary. At frequent intervals, an evaluation of the progress made to date should be attempted. Again, flexibility in organisation is important and allowance should be made for changes of interest and growing new interests to emerge.

The project should not be extended beyond its sphere of usefulness.

The following example illustrates how a small project can be prepared. It will be seen that the plan incorporates the suggestions outlined in Chapter 5, i.e. lesson 1 is devoted to introducing the topic, lesson 2 develops the topic, and lesson 3 continues and concludes the work.

SUBJECT: History Project.   *The Story of Food.*
CLASS: 30 children.   AGE: 8 +.
LESSONS: 3 of 50 minutes.
AIM: To exercise the children's skills in acquiring and using information, and to aid the growth of their concepts of time and development by examining the story of popular foodstuffs.

LESSON I

Introduction (a) Discuss, perhaps with genuine examples, a typical meal consisting of :

1. Chicken.
2. Mashed potatoes.
3. Tinned peas.
4. Apple pie.
5. Ice-cream.
6. Coffee.

Point out that each of these items has its own story.

(b) Divide the 30 children into six groups of five, one group to each item. Provide each group with a prepared sheet of information concerning that item.

(c) Invite the children to study the information, and divide the story of each foodstuff into five stages, one for each child in the group.

LESSON 2

Development Each group will construct a series of five small tableaux—one child to each tableau—illustrating the five stages chosen in the story of the foodstuff, e.g.

> *The Story of Apple-pie:*
> 1. Remains of apples in Central European lake-dwellings.
> 2. Romans bringing apples to Britain.
> 3. Pilgrim Fathers taking apple trees to America.
> 4. Granny Smith in New Zealand.
> 5. Growing, harvesting, importing, retailing and cooking the apple.

LESSON 3

Continuation (*a*) Children to arrange the sets of tableaux in exhibition form, preferably in circular shape, with the 'meal' at the centre, and each series moving in towards it.

(*b*) Group leaders to narrate and guide the rest of the class through each story in turn, showing and describing information, pictures, examples, etc., which the group has collected.

CHAPTER SEVEN

General Conduct in Schools

Relationship with the Head Teacher

Schools exist primarily for the purpose of educating children, and not for the sole purpose of providing 'guinea pigs' on which students can experiment. The school has a permanent life of its own against which the arrival of the student on a school practice is but a short and transitory intrusion.

The head teacher enjoys a unique position in the British school. He is totally responsible for what goes on in his school, and his position might be compared with that of the captain of a ship. He will have obtained his office by virtue of his professional experience and qualities of leadership. Because he has been elected to this responsible position he deserves respect.

Within his school, the head teacher's authority is supreme. He is in no way subordinate to the wishes of a college of education, although most heads go out of their way to accommodate and co-operate with the colleges in the interests of the students.

Nevertheless, all visitors to the school, other than the appointed staff of the school, enter it by invitation, i.e. as guests. The student on school practice is a particularly difficult guest, for during his stay the courtesy extended to him by the head and his staff is an addition to their full-time work of administration and routine teaching.

Students' demands and requests will inevitably and rightly be subordinated to the needs of the children and the members of the staff. The head's position of authority gives him the clearest and most experienced understanding of these needs.

Relationship with the Class Teacher

In the primary school the student will probably find himself working with the class teacher for the greater part of his stay in the school. Even at the secondary school stage, where the student may be taking specialist subjects, he will probably be assigned to one member of the staff who will be responsible, under the head teacher, for his progress. The harmony of this relationship will have a considerable effect on the benefit that can be derived from the school practice.

The object of the school practice is to learn how to teach. Considering the relationship between the class teacher and the student, we might repeat the analogy used in Chapter One, of the craftsman and the apprentice and their respective roles. The student will find that most class teachers, if approached in the proper way, will be only too willing and happy to offer advice.

This harmonious relationship can be destroyed by sheer thoughtlessness on the part of the student. The following list contains some useful DON'TS for the student:

(*a*) DON'T reorganise the routine administration of the class without the permission of the teacher. The class teacher may have spent two or three months establishing a routine which works best for him and best for the class. A student can disrupt this in three days. The teacher's established routine might embrace such activities as collecting, storing and issuing equipment and books, children entering the classroom, etc.

(*b*) DON'T alter the arrangement of the furniture in the classroom without the permission of the teacher. Most teachers give considerable thought to such details, and will usually have very good reasons, based on their superior knowledge of the children, for the arrangement they have.

(*c*) DON'T lose the equipment of the class. This is usually on the teacher's inventory. Footballs, standard P.E. apparatus, text books, etc. are often difficult to obtain and may have been accumulated slowly and patiently over long periods.

(*d*) DON'T lower the class teacher's standards. It is the normal practice in schools to demand that work written in pupils' exercise books should be their best work. The high standards obtained are the result of constant attention to detail, and vigilance on the part of the teacher. Such standards of work are easier to lose than to restore.

(*e*) DON'T relax the rules of the classroom. If the teacher insists that the children are to go out of the classroom during play-times, the student must do the same. If the teacher insists on the children entering and leaving the classroom in an orderly manner, it is the job of the student to sustain this rule.

(*f*) DON'T ask for equipment or help from the class teacher at the last minute. He has other things to do besides looking after the student.

(*g*) DON'T deviate from the marking systems or methods which are agreed upon by the staff. These schemes have been produced after careful thought and deliberation, and are known to the children. To alter or amend is to invite confusion.

(h) DON'T allow a parade of children to the staff room during the break-time. This is the teachers' period of rest. For the children to intrude upon it is a common cause of irritation.

(i) DON'T leave exercise books unmarked. If the student has set the work, then he should mark it.

We could add to this list of DON'Ts. The essential point to bear in mind is that the student on school practice should try to appreciate the work of looking after a class from the class teacher's point of view. The student does not always reap the consequences of his stay in school. The class teacher has to continue from where the student has left off. 'The assistant (teacher) is keen. He has struggled hard to enable his class to reach a certain level of work and behaviour. He has striven to secure a standard and a method which in his opinion are essentially right. The results he has obtained have come by constant insistence on the chosen ideal. That being the case, he is a little fearful about the well-meant but not very efficient efforts of the visitor from outside. And it must be recognised that a mediocre student can do much damage to a class. The sad part of the story is that the student just doesn't realise the chaos he creates.'*

Relationship with the Pupils

'The essence of the pupil-teacher relationship is that the

* K. M. Roach *I Want to Teach* (U.L.P.) p. 28.

teacher is in authority, and the pupil under authority.'*
While on school practice the student takes over the
responsibilities and authority of the teacher. This is not
an easy task. It may be made more difficult by the obvious
youth of the student, and also by the attitude of the
children who might adopt the 'he's only a student'
approach. This situation, if and when it arises, must be
met. The student should at all times be firm but kindly.
He should insist on the pupils' addressing him in the same
way as they address members of the school staff. Even in
the most democratic social climate he is still the leader,
the most mature and responsible person in the room. He
cannot morally abdicate this position. He should know
what is best for the children and have the courage to act
on this knowledge.

Professional Attitude and Commitments

During his school practice the student will be assuming
the role of an established member of the profession.
Membership of this profession carries with it a code of
ethics and obligations. The student should remember
that his contacts with other members of staff should at all
times be in accordance with these established rules of
conduct.

One of the obligations, assumed by teachers, is that of
providing proper and adequate supervision of their
charges. The student should do likewise.

All members of staff are equally responsible for en-
forcing those rules and regulations which are laid down

* T. E. A. Verity *On Becoming a Teacher* (U.L.P.) p. 55.

for the benefit of all. The student should not avoid taking action when it is called for.

Throughout his stay in the school the student should conduct himself in a manner which is consistent with the dignity of a noble and responsible profession. If the student is to get the most out of his school practice he must involve himself in the activities and affairs of the school. He should take a real interest in the children and in their extra-curricular and extra-mural activities. He should involve himself willingly, without supervision, not merely with his own success in view, but because he wishes to make an effort that is worthy of him.

Moral and Legal Responsibilities

When a parent sends his child to school he is placing a great deal of the responsibility of educating the child in the hands of others. He has a right to expect this implicit trust to be honoured. The responsibilities of the class teacher or student are not, therefore, to be taken lightly. They are dealing with impressionable 'material'. The student has a moral responsibility to do his very best for the children in his care. Half-hearted efforts do not only affect the student himself but all those with whom he comes into contact. To do only sufficient to scrape through a school practice or survive until the end of the period, is morally indefensible.

The student also has a legal responsibility. The following statement prepared by Kenneth Wormald, O.B.E., B.A., Solicitor to the National Union of Teachers, presents an authoritative opinion regarding the legal position of students on school practice:

'Students on Teaching Practice.

'The Head of a School, under the Articles of Government or Rules of Management, is responsible for the internal organisation, management and discipline, and, by virtue of his or her position, controls the teaching and non-teaching staff. When the student, therefore, is on the School premises on teaching practice, he is under the immediate control of the Head with regard to all his professional work.

'The Head, however, acts through the qualified staff, particularly the Heads of Department, and the student's main contact might well be with the Head of Department and finally the particular class teacher.

'I assume, therefore, that it is unlikely that at the outset a student on school practice will take a class without an experienced teacher being present. The experienced teacher would ensure that the student is only given such responsibilities as he or she can reasonably be expected to accept, in the light of his or her experience and capabilities. The trained teacher will assess the student's capabilities and, presumably, will gradually give him or her greater scope with a class.

'In the case of teachers, the law regards them as being *in loco parentis* to the pupils in their care. That means they would be required to exercise that standard of care towards their pupils that would be expected of a reasonably careful parent.

'The student, when he comes to the School, is not a qualified teacher, and I think it is unlikely that the Courts would regard him in the same light as a fully qualified teacher. Consequently, when a student is introduced to a class, the teacher in charge will not completely delegate his authority to the student, and the ultimate responsibility for the safety and care of the pupils would, therefore, rest with the teacher in charge of the class.

'Provided the student acts in accordance with the advice of the teacher, and only uses recognised methods of teaching, such as are currently used in schools, according to the dictates of reasonably minded practitioners, there should be little likelihood of the student being held legally liable should a pupil be unfortunately injured whilst the student is taking the class. The student, although not *in loco parentis* to the pupil, would, nevertheless, be expected by the Courts to exercise the standard of care of a reasonable man towards the pupils in the class. It must be emphasised, however, that so far as legal liability for an accident to a pupil is concerned, this could only be placed upon a student if it could be established that the student had in some way acted negligently or carelessly and as a result of that negligence or carelessness the pupil had been injured. If a pupil is injured as a result of a pure accident, no legal liability for compensation would fall upon any person or persons. Neither the student nor the teacher in charge of the class, therefore, is automatically responsible should one of the pupils be injured.

'So far as the question of discipline is concerned, a teacher, by reason of the fact that he is *in loco parentis* to the pupils, is entitled at common law to chastise them reasonably. A student, however, I think, would probably be regarded in a different position, and it is important, therefore, for the student to leave any corporal punishment of the pupils to the qualified teachers, and, indeed, not on any occasion to use any violence towards his pupils. If a student does have occasion to strike a pupil, this would be an assault, and it is doubtful whether he could rely on the defence available to qualified teachers, that he was acting in accordance with his common law right as a teacher to chastise the pupil reasonably. So far as non-corporal punishments are concerned, the student should be guided at all times by the teacher in charge of his class, the Head of the Department and the Head Teacher, and should not endeavour to exceed any instructions in this respect given to him by the qualified teachers.

'The practical point, so far as students on teaching practice are concerned, is that they should at all times ensure that they conform to the pattern of the School to which they are sent, and remember that the guidance of experienced teachers is always available to them if in difficulties.

'So far as members of the National Union of Teachers are concerned, and this includes student associate members, the full legal protection of the Union is afforded in any case of any legal claim being made against a teacher by a pupil, and also for a member, should he or she have grounds for a claim against any person arising out of an injury incurred during the course of his or her professional duties.'

Fitting into the Scheme

The student should contribute to the established harmony of the school. The tone associated with good schools is not an accident. It has been created, nurtured and fostered over the years. The student should try to add to its strength, not leave it weaker. This requires deliberate thought. The best administration is usually the most unobtrusive and economical, and usually the friendliest and most harmonious.

It may well be difficult for the student to compromise for the greater good of the whole. It may be difficult for him to come to terms with the practices and the methods he sees in use if they are markedly different from those with which he is familiar through his lectures and college instruction.

'Compromise is not disloyalty. The person who holds views with the rigidity of cast iron and refuses to bend, can be a source of unending trouble in any community of which he is a member . . . With the interests of the community, common-room, or the whole school at heart, it is possible and often indeed desirable to allow oneself to be persuaded to a course of action which one would never have taken from personal choice. Humility and toleration are not un-Christian virtues.'*

General Conduct

The head teacher of the school will expect the student teacher to accept the same obligations as the remainder of the staff, and he is entitled to see that these are fulfilled. He will expect his members of staff to be punctual and, wherever possible, to give good warning of proposed absence so that he can make proper alternative arrangements. He will expect them to be properly dressed and set a standard of appearance which will serve as an example to the children.

* T. E. A. Verity *On Becoming a Teacher* (U.L.P.) p. 73.

CHAPTER EIGHT

Evaluating Your Teaching

While there is no generally accepted formula or universal method used in colleges of education to evaluate lessons, there does exist a considerable degree of agreement between them as to what criteria are relevant.

There are obviously several generally accepted elements which can be observed and recognised in a good lesson. This chapter lists some of the factors which a supervisor might consider, and which can therefore be used by the student as a means of self-evaluation. Any of the following aspects of the lesson might provide scope for improvement and progress, and might be the object of advice or comment from supervisors.

Relationship with the Children

Climate. Effective learning is unlikely to take place in an atmosphere of distrust, fear, anxiety or contempt. The student must therefore endeavour to create a climate in the classroom that is conducive to enthusiastic and pleasurable co-operation.

Friendliness. The student should be friendly without being either patronising or familiar in his relations with the children. 'The teacher should maintain a friendly attitude to his pupils; but it is unwise to be too chatty or "big-brotherly"—especially at first ... it is advisable to be a little inscrutable for a while at the start. Gradually you will win the confidence of your pupils without losing their respect; and then it is possible to be friendly and open on both sides without fear of abuse. That situation is one of the most delightful of experiences, and it is the schoolmaster's great reward.'[*]

Mutual respect. The relationship between the teacher and pupil should be one of mutual respect, in that the good teacher respects and is considerate of the feelings and individuality of each pupil.

Discipline. He should, nevertheless, exercise an effective control of the situation. '. . . the individual teacher has also both the authority for "keeping order", and the duty of securing it, as far as his own personal relations with his pupils are concerned.'[†]

Personal Manner

'Children are strict assessors. Even before he speaks a teacher may betray himself.'[‡]

It has been found that among the personal traits which have a high correlation with efficiency on school practice were poise, self-confidence and enthusiasm. Those traits associated with weakness in practice teaching were bashfulness, hesitancy, listlessness, reserve and self-distrust.[§]

Authority. On a school practice the student in charge of the class is in a position of authority. This does not mean that authority is equated with domination, nor does it mean that he should retreat into the background and

[*] H. C. Barnard *An Introduction to Teaching* (U.L.P.) p. 150.
[†] Ibid. p. 153.
[‡] Davies and Shepherd *Teaching: Begin Here* (Epworth Press) p. 59.
[§] See H. Bowers *Research in the Teaching of Teachers* (Dent and Sons (Canada) Ltd.).

abdicate from his position of responsibility. There are many excellent texts which deal with the question of a democratic social climate in teaching and the proper use of authority. Some of these are mentioned in the Select Bibliography (Appendix A).

Enthusiasm. Enthusiasm is infectious. If the student wishes his children to be enthusiastic he must accept the need to communicate this enthusiasm to them.

Permissiveness. The quality of the student's ability will be reflected in the degree of freedom he can reasonably permit.

Mannerisms. Personal mannerisms on the part of the student should be avoided when they are likely to intrude upon, or distract from, the content of the lesson. Such mannerisms may affect speech, or may be the result of nervousness and take the form of physical gestures. Many are difficult to eradicate and will need deliberate self-discipline on the part of the student.

Organisation and Analysis of Subject-Matter

These are dealt with in Chapters Three and Four on schemes of work and lesson note preparation, and the student would be well advised to consult these chapters. Comment, criticism and improvement might in this case take place before the actual lesson is given .

Adequacy of notes. Adequate preparation of lesson notes helps good control and efficient teaching. The student who has prepared well usually enters the classroom ready and confident to tackle the job and to cope with most eventualities. Slap-dash, casual and indifferent preparation, where not enough time and thought have been given, is usually associated with teaching of a low standard.

Suitability. Lesson notes will be evaluated in terms of their suitability to the needs, age, ability and readiness of the children for whom they are prepared.

Logical sequence. Both the scheme of work and the notes of the lesson itself should show a logical analysis and development of subject-matter.

Relevance. Isolated bits and pieces of information which possess little continuity and connection with the aim of the lesson are indicative of inadequate care and thought in the preparation. The learning experiences should be significant, worthwhile and a unity in themselves.

Interest. One of the most important facts that the student should bear in mind in all his lessons is that if the subject is not interesting to the children it is his responsibility to try to make it so.

Originality. While originality is not in itself a virtue, and in many cases may be inappropriate, the student should search out means to infuse variety and imagination into his work.

Challenge. If the work attempted by the children is to be interesting and meaningful to them, it must prove a challenge. A standard of work that is too easy, or constant repetition, may degenerate into sheer drudgery. The best learning, however, will result when the pupils are actively pursuing knowledge to satisfy needs of which they are aware. That is the research attitude—the attitude of all who strike out on their own into new territory. One cannot, of course, expect every child to be a daring pioneer, but one should, at least, give every child the opportunity of discovering his particular bent and of feeling that he is indeed exploring.'*

Presentation of Subject-Matter

Adaptability. Generally speaking, frequent deviation from prepared notes will suggest inadequate original preparation. Nevertheless, the student should be sensitive to the needs of the moment and be prepared to adjust his teaching to the prevailing climate of the classroom.

Stimulation. The methods employed to communicate the subject-matter should be stimulating and provocative to the children.

Instruction. At the conclusion of the lesson the children should either know more or in some way have benefited from the experience. This would seem to be the acid test of whether learning has taken place and whether, in fact, the lesson was worth giving. While this may be difficult to evaluate immediately in all cases, it is nonetheless a worth-while and useful criterion to apply.

Response of the Children

Interest and enthusiasm. The quality of the children's response to the lesson will be indicative of the success with which the previously mentioned factors and principles have been applied.

Activity. 'Any organism abhors inactivity.'† The fact that the student cannot do the learning for the children, although self-evident, is not always fully appreciated by the novice. The pupils should be actively engaged at all

* G. P. Kellaway *Purposeful Education* (U.L.P.).

† W. H. Kilpatrick *Philosophy of Education* (Macmillan, New York, 1951) p. 13.

times. Some part of most lessons will normally be given up to pupil activity. It is a common fault of the beginner to do too much for the children instead of encouraging them to do things for themselves. 'It is important to stress, however, that we are here concerned only with activity as an integral and balanced part of the process of total education, not as a fitful and uncertain adjunct. As a properly planned method, activity should give direction to learning at every stage of education, and should not be the prerogative of the research worker.'*

General Techniques of Teaching

There are many techniques which can be used in any teaching situation. There is no obligation or necessity to use these general techniques on every occasion, but when they are employed they will be subject to criticism by those who assess the lesson.

Organisation. Lessons vary in the amount of organisation that is involved. Woodwork, Craft, Art and Domestic Science, for example, usually require a complicated arrangement and distribution of equipment. Drama lessons, P.E. and Country Dancing, on the other hand, may need careful organisation of pupils, space and equipment.

The way in which this organisation is carried out will greatly affect the student's control and the discipline of the class. There are very many suggestions and techniques to be found which are constantly being practised by experienced teachers. The student would do well to take note of these and learn to apply as many as possible.

Voice. The voice of the teacher is the primary means of

* G. P. Kellaway *Purposeful Education* (U.L.P.) p. 44.

communication in teaching. Its effective use involves variation of tone, clarity of expression, an enthusiastic quality, and it should be sufficiently loud to be heard by all children in the classroom. Common faults that the student should avoid are monotonous delivery and shouting.

The blackboard. Despite many modern improvements in facilities and mechanical aids the blackboard remains the principal visual aid of the classroom. The student's illustrations should be clear and relevant and his writing neat and legible. Blackboard work can often be prepared before the lesson takes place. Spelling mistakes and inaccuracies found on students' blackboards are a constant source of irritation to serving teachers and college of education supervisors.

Mechanical and visual aids. The student needs no reminding that children learn better through multi-sensory experiences. Visual, audio and mechanical aids make learning more effective and permanent. Again, there are techniques of using these aids, and the student should know them. There is no intrinsic virtue, however, in using complicated apparatus, and its relevance to the task in hand should always be considered.

Questioning. 'Nothing does more to differentiate the novice from the experienced teacher than this ability to use oral questioning effectively.'* The power to question well has been described as 'one of the fine arts of teaching', an art which is only acquired by painstaking and persistent practice. It is not surprising, therefore, that the inexperienced student invariably shows considerable

* Davies and Shepherd *Teaching: Begin Here* (Epworth Press) p. 87.

weaknesses in questioning, and the poor response he receives from the children is often due to the ill-prepared, unsuitable, ambiguous and irrelevant questions which he asks.

Yet it is commonplace to find students on school practice who record in their lesson notes that 'the teacher will begin by asking questions'—as though this can be done by the beginner on the spur of the moment and without due thought and preparation beforehand. 'The value of being able to question well is undoubted, and it is well worth-while to pay special attention to the matter from the beginning, for weakness in questioning is almost universal with beginners and greatly retards general improvement and efficiency.'*

In evaluating the worth of a lesson, the supervisor will consider the ability shown by the student in using the technique of oral questioning. The student should become skilled in this technique as soon as possible—and this means thought, preparation, practice and experiment for the beginner.

The following points are intended for the guidance of the student in preparing and using questioning effectively in his lessons.

1. Before the Lesson

In the initial stages of preparing a lesson, the student should consider:

(a) The particular aim of the lesson and to what extent questions are needed to achieve this aim.

* F. M. Austin *The Art of Questioning in the Classroom* (U.L.P.) preface, p. ix.

(*b*) The number of questions to be asked, bearing in mind that the number of questions will depend on the kind of lesson. In the typical Appreciation lesson, for example, the worth-while emotional or aesthetic reaction which the student seeks may be destroyed by the interposing of too many questions .

(*c*) Where and how in the lesson will the questions be introduced? Which parts of the lesson will require many questions, which parts few?

(*d*) The most important reason for asking questions is to help the children to think. Questions intended primarily to stimulate thought are 'teaching' questions and should lead children to make observations and to draw inferences for themselves. 'Teaching' questions require special care and attention, and should always be prepared before the lesson begins. They are intended to make the pupils follow a certain course of thought, planned by the teacher, and aimed at a definite goal. Very often the whole meaning of a certain part of the lesson will depend on the use made of skilful 'teaching' questions which help the children to deduce and reason for themselves. Poor questioning may easily ruin the lesson at this stage.

2. During the Lesson

While the lesson is in progress, questioning can help the student in the following ways:

(*a*) To find out what the children know.

(*b*) To revise and remind the children of previous work they have done. Questions often serve to introduce the lesson. Such questions are frequently referred to as 'testing' questions, and the student should appreciate the difference between a 'teaching' question and a 'testing' question and he should know how to use both kinds.

(c) To arouse the curiosity of the pupils, thereby creating a receptive intellectual and emotional climate in the classroom.

(d) To create in the classroom a stimulating and challenging atmosphere which is conducive to good learning and good work.

(e) To maintain the interest and effort of the children.

(f) To find out whether the pupils understand what is being taught.

(g) To encourage the children to think for themselves and to reason.

(h) To evaluate the results of the teaching.

(i) To discover what he has taught well, and whether the methods employed have been successful or unsuccessful. In other words, questions test not only the children's learning, but also the student's teaching.

3. After the Lesson

To become more skilled in the art of questioning, the student should learn to evaluate the success he has had in his lessons. He might ask himself the following questions:

(a) Considering the aim of the lesson, how successful were the questions in achieving this aim?

(b) Some of the questions were unsuccessful. Why?

(c) Why did certain questions receive no answer at all? Why did some need repeating? modifying? abandoning?

(d) Why did some questions produce unexpected answers?

(e) Were the children bored by too many questions?

(*f*) Did the questions asked prove interesting to the children? How many children tried to answer the questions?

(*g*) Were the questions clearly phrased? Were they relevant to the age and interests of the class?

4. Hints on Questioning

(*a*) Marks of good questioning are clarity, economy in words, leading straight to the point, requiring only short answers, having only one right answer.

(*b*) Vague questions should be avoided. For example, 'Can anyone tell me about Malaya?'

(*c*) Questions should usually be addressed to individuals to avoid simultaneous answering.

(*d*) Wrong answers should not be ignored. The student should endeavour to cultivate the art of turning wrong answers into right.

(*e*) Children should be given opportunities to ask questions of the teacher.*

(*f*) The student's questions should not interrupt or disturb the children's thinking.

* In *Questioning in the Classroom* p. 35, F. M. Austin, writing on 'Children's Questions', uses the following table to record the number of questions asked by students in a series of lessons and the number of questions asked by the class:

Duration of lesson	Subject	Number of questions asked by student	Number of questions asked by class
35 minutes	Geography	56	2
40 minutes	Arithmetic	84	0
40 minutes	Reading	23	0
40 minutes	Nature study	55	3
40 minutes	Geometry	57	3
etc.			

(g) Questioning has an important place in the lesson, but the student should be cautioned about asking too many questions, or too few, or using questions at the wrong time in the lesson.

Versatility. No matter how well prepared the student may be, situations which have not been anticipated are certain to arise in the normal course of everyday events in the classroom. These may momentarily cause panic. The degree with which a student can respond to the unpredictable will be a measure of his personal poise and technical maturity.

Estimation of Progress in Teaching Ability

The acquisition of teaching technique requires experience, practice, reflection, discipline and training. It will not come easily or early. To become a skilled teacher with a mature and comprehensive technique probably takes years. The student should remember that his supervisors are well aware of his inexperience and apprentice-status, and that they will take this into account in their estimation of his worth and promise as a teacher. The main criterion which will be applied will be progress in the use of the skills of teaching.

The skill of the student as a teacher will naturally be expected to be more developed and mature on a final school practice than on earlier practices.

CHAPTER NINE

How to get the Best out of Your Teaching Practice

For some students teaching practice is something to be survived rather than enjoyed. To pretend that it is easy would be naïve and foolish. Teaching is a difficult art to practise, but it is one that can be learned through application, patience and diligence. Teaching practice is that part of the student's training which is most like the real thing, and in this sense it is the most dramatic and important part of his course of training. He should approach it in a positive way as an opportunity to experiment, discover and to develop his knowledge and appreciation of the problems involved in the job of teaching.

Observing Children at Work and Play

All the Psychology, Philosophy, Principles, Techniques and Methods learned by the student in the course of academic lectures cannot be complete until they are translated into teaching and related to *children*. Teaching practice may be the first occasion on which some students are faced with the need for understanding children. Children are not adults and do not behave like them; nor is the behaviour of children in school like their behaviour at home and elsewhere.

Learning is associated with behaving and involves

changes in behaviour. By observation of the natural behaviour of children the student gains deeper insight into and understanding of the children he will teach.

Observation does not simply mean 'looking at' children. It needs to be done systematically and deliberately with the object of finding out why children behave as they do; what makes them change; in fact, what makes them 'tick'. There are some students who may remain inadequate for the whole of their professional lives simply because they just do not know about children—they will never take the trouble to observe them.

Observation should not be confined to the classroom. Children behave differently in different circumstances and situations. They respond in one way to one person or situation, and in another way to another person or situation. It is these differences and the reasons for them which provide the student with a clear picture of the whole child in his many roles. This is tremendously important in helping the student to understand the meaning of individual differences.

Learning from Experienced Practitioners

Besides the importance of observing children, school practice provides an ideal opportunity not only to observe the 'raw material' of education, but to watch it being cultivated by the craftsman. The student can get a practical illustration of a great many of the methods and techniques which he has heard about, by watching the experienced practitioner. Reference has already been made (Chapter 2, page 18) to some of the important factors involved in the teacher–class relationship.

Self-criticism

Most colleges of education recommend their students to make some form of personal evaluation of each lesson they give and include this in their own lesson notes file. There are good reasons for this:

1. It helps the student to recognise his own faults shortcomings and omissions, and in doing this he is more than half-way to overcoming them.

2. 'It has already been stressed that a teacher must go on learning and improving during the whole of his career. To do this it is necessary that he should be able to criticise his own lessons accurately.'*

When the student finishes his professional training and enters the classroom as a qualified teacher, there will be few opportunities for him to observe other teachers. He will, generally speaking, receive little supervision or assistance. In most cases he will have to work out his own salvation, and it is important, therefore, that early in his career he should get into the habit of examining himself critically as a teacher.

When writing critical comments on lessons, the student should consider the following suggestions:

1. Comments should be written as soon as possible after the completion of the lesson.

2. The comments should be specific and directed at a critical evaluation of the content, methods and techniques employed. For example, a typical comment of a student is 'the class seemed to respond very well'. A more fruitful comment, showing more critical evaluation, would be

* H. J. Byrne *The Teacher and his Pupils* (Oxford) p. 41.

'the class seemed to respond better to Stage 1 of the Development method than to Stage 4'. This kind of comment *must* lead the student to ask himself why one method or section was more effective than another.

3. The comment should embody a therapeutic element. It should offer suggestions for improvement, or explanations of mistakes that can be avoided in the future.

Conclusion

Day by day the teacher's technical ability develops; new experiences are encountered, new experiments handled, new evaluations made. The end of school practice is a milestone on the path towards professional maturity. The fusion of personality with professional skill, knowledge and technique has begun, and should never end.

SELECT BIBLIOGRAPHY OF BOOKS ON TEACHING METHOD

The following books are recommended for their significance and value as an aid to students on school practice. They are all 'general method' text books dealing with the whole question of learning and teaching. We have drawn attention to those sections which we consider relevant to the theme of this book.

Communications and Learning in the Primary School by L. G. W. Sealey and Vivian Gibbon (Blackwell).

This book is particularly valuable for its treatment of the content of the curriculum of the primary school as an integrated whole, using language work as its focus.

Effective Teaching by R. A. Oliver (J. M. Dent & Sons (Canada) Ltd.).

This book is primarily concerned with practical methods of teaching. Much sound advice is offered on the following school practice problems:
The structure of lessons; types of lessons; specimen lesson notes; projects and units of work; questioning; and the use of visual aids.

The Foundations of Education by W. F. Connell et al. (Cresset Press)

This important book offers a great deal of useful advice

to student teachers. Of particular relevance to the teaching practice situation are:

Chapter 11—The Fundamentals of Teaching Method
Chapter 12—Group and Individual Methods
Chapter 13—Classroom Management and Discipline

Inside the Primary School by John Blackie (H. M. S. O.).

This is a useful introduction to the new methods and attitudes that are developing in primary schools. Chapter five, 'The curriculum the timetable and organisation', is the most immediately relevant for students about to embark on teaching practice.

Teaching: Begin Here by W. T. Davies & T. B. Shepherd (Epworth Press).

The first half of this book, particularly Chapters 4 to 10, is well worth reading in preparation for school practice. Especially valuable are the lesson plan layouts and the chapters devoted to advice to the teacher in front of his class.

Techniques of Teaching Volume 1 Primary Education edited by A. D. C. Peterson (Pergamon Press).

This book is in four parts. The first chapter deals with the social education of infants. Especially valuable to students are chapters 2 and 3 which deal with reading and numbers.

The Treasure Chest for Teachers by the N.U.T. (Schoolmaster Publishing Co.).

This inexpensive booklet offers information about educational associations, embassies, consulates, travel agencies, and industrial and commercial organisations which offer certain services and supply teaching materials free, or at reduced rates, for the use of schools and training colleges. Addresses are included.

The booklet gives details of the services offered and the literature, films and film-strips which are provided by these various agencies. This book would be a valuable asset to those students who wish to supplement the routine material provided by the schools in which they practise with extra material which might make their lessons distinctive.

PROFESSIONAL SOURCES OF ADVICE AND INFORMATION

Many students on teaching practice remain unaware of the numerous sources of professional and semi-official assistance they might use. The following is a list of periodicals, books and facilities which are specially provided to assist the practising teacher in obtaining information, or to help him improve his methods of teaching. These facilities are equally available to the student on school practice.

The Teacher (published weekly by the Schoolmaster Publishing Co. Ltd., Hamilton House, Hastings Street, London W.C.2).

This is the official organ of the National Union of Teachers. It contains regular weekly features on the teaching of general subjects in Infants, Junior and Secondary schools, as well as articles of general professional interest and those concerned with Union matters.

The Times Educational Supplement (published weekly by Times Newspapers Ltd., New Printing House Square, Gray's Inn Road, London W.C.1).

This journal contains articles on current educational problems and topics, reports on contemporary trends in education at home and abroad, and, of particular use to the student, reviews of the latest books published in the educational field.

The Teacher's World (published weekly by Evans Bros., Montague House, Russell Square, London W.C.1).

This publication is devoted almost entirely to methods and original practical suggestions which are of great value to the serving teacher.

Visual Education (published monthly by the National Committee for Audio and Visual Aids in Education, 33 Queen Anne Street, London W.1).

This magazine contains articles on the use of visual aids in the various subjects, and methods of making such aids. It also contains details of sources of equipment and material.

Child Education (published monthly by Evans Bros., Montague House, Russell Square, London W.C.1).

This caters mainly for the Infants and Lower Junior age group, and contains stories, songs, plays, poems, games, ideas for teaching art, English, etc., to the very young.

Public Libraries

In the larger towns and cities special facilities are provided for teachers by the library authorities. This service usually extends to the loan of sets of text books, often on a long-term basis. It sometimes includes loan of charts, diagrams, and specimens (ornithological, botanical, geological, etc.). It may also offer films, film-strips and records or tapes.

Local Education Authorities

Many LEAs have throughout the years built up their own film-strip, film and professional teachers' libraries. Details of the facilities provided by these are usually obtainable in the school. Very often film projectors and other specialised equipment can be borrowed from official sources if adequate notice is given. Students should also remember that organisers employed by the LEAs are able to offer additional help and advice in these matters.

Museums and Art Galleries

Most museums have a children's section, or are prepared to co-operate with schools in providing loan collections or by accommodating groups of school children on visits. Many museums and galleries will provide guides, and in some cases may have teachers on their staffs to assist serving teachers with their special requirements.

The School Broadcasting Council

In addition to the broadsheets announcing times of programmes broadcast to schools, the B.B.C. provides pamphlets for use in connection with these broadcasts. Most subjects are adequately catered for, both in Primary and Secondary Schools. Many schools retain pamphlets after use, and these may prove a very valuable source of information and illustration for the student teacher.

SOURCES OF TEACHING AIDS

Teaching aids, films and film-strips can be borrowed or purchased from the following sources.

I. BEVERAGES AND CONFECTIONARY

Brazilian Embassy (Coffee), 33 Green Street, London W1. Free copies of booklets on coffee.

Brooke Bond Oxo, Education Service, Department CB, Leon House, High Street, Croydon, Surrey CR9 1JQ. 'Story of Tea' book free to teachers. Sets of previous picture card series 12½p per set.

Cadbury Bros. Ltd, Schools Department Bournville. Wallcharts, wall friezes, books and demonstration samples on cocoa growing, and cocoa and chocolate production, available to teachers at small charges.

Ceylon Tea Centre, Education Department, 22 Regent Street, London SW1. Wall pictures, maps, pictorial cards, booklets, project material, filmstrips, on sale. Films on free loan.

Coffee Promotion Council, 10 Eastcheap, London EC3. Wallcharts and booklets free on request.

Colombian Embassy (Coffee), 31 Hans Crescent, London SW1. Free booklets.

Kenya Coffee Industry, 248 Grand Buildings, Trafalgar Square, London WC2. Booklets and samples free.

National Dairy Council, John Princes Street, London W1M OAP. Catalogue of booklets, leaflets, charts, teachers' notes and filmstrips. Films available on free loan.

The Nestle Co. Ltd, Educational Aids Department, Great Castle Street, London W1. Wallchart project box, colour filmstrip with teaching notes illustrating the manufacturing process of milk chocolate. Booklets on the Story of Chocolate and the Story of Coffee supplied free on request.

Rowntrees, Cocoa Works, York. Typescript available free on cocoa and chocolate. Display case (sometimes free) – Raw Cocoa, Shell, Nibs, Butter, etc.

2. COMMODITIES

Bananas, Elders and Fyffe, Publicity Manager, 15 Stratton Street, Piccadilly, London W1A 2LL. Free copies of booklet 'The Fruit of the Wise Man'.

Birds Eye Foods Ltd, Education Mailing Service, 177 Hook Road, Surbiton, Surrey. Free booklets in quantity, also wallcharts and recipe cards.

Bowaters Paper Corporation Ltd, Public Relations Offices, Bowater House, Knightsbridge, London SW1. Booklet for teachers and films on free loan.

Brown and Polson Ltd (Knorr), Product Publicity Centre, 10 New Fetter Lane, London EC4. Wallcharts available at low cost.

Dunlop Rubber Co. Ltd, 10/12 King Street, St James's, London SW1. Free distribution of booklets and samples in Great Britain and Northern Ireland.

Educational Productions Ltd, East Ardsley, Wakefield, Yorks. Many varying publications for sale or hire – material usually provided in conjunction with organisations named in this section.

The Flour Advisory Bureau, 21 Arlington Street, London SW1. Supplies literature on wheat, flour and flour milling (including samples from milling processes) and notes on baking.

Goodyear Tyres, Public Relations Department, Wolverhampton. Free booklets available.

Heinz Home Cookery Service, Hayes Park, Hayes, Middlesex. Workcards, booklets, flannelgraph for purchase.

Imperial Tobacco Co., Imperial House, 1 Grosvenor Place, London SW1. Booklets on crisps, baked beans, table sauces.

Macaroni Advisory Bureau, c/o Quaker Oats Ltd, Southall,

APPENDIX C

Middlesex. Macaroni Filmstrip 'Tricks and Treats with Macaroni', together with narration guide and appropriate recipe leaflets available.

McDougalls Ltd, Janet Johnson, Wheatsheaf Mills, London E14. Illustrated booklet 'The Story of a Bag of Flour', samples of wheat and flour, all free of charge, but maximum 50 copies each per school. Project Box of Wheat-to-Flour samples for sale.

Natural Rubber Producers Research Association, 19 Buckingham Street, London WC2N 6EJ. Class set of booklets entitled 'Story of Natural Rubber' and leaflets.

New Zealand Dairy Production and Marketing Board, St Olaf House, Tooley Street, London SE1. Free books available on dairy farming, butter and cheese.

Potato Marketing Board, 50 Hans Crescent, Knightsbridge, London SW1. A four-page illustrated news-sheet is available free giving full particulars of material available for purchase.

Quaker Oats Ltd, Sales Promotion Department, Southall, Middlesex. Leaflet on milling processes of oats and recipe books available on request.

Ranks Hovis McDougall Ltd, Public Relations Department, 53 Eastcheap, London EC3. Colour folder and booklets on bread-baking etc. Colour film (16mm., 25 minutes) on commercial bread-baking available on free loan.

Reed Paper Group, Educational Services Department, 82 Baker Street, London W1. Booklet in class sets, samples set and films on loan.

Tate & Lyle (Sugar), Educational Aids Bureau, 21 Mincing Lane, London EC3. Sample display card, pamphlet and booklet available free.

Timber Research and Development Association, St John's Road, Tylers Green, High Wycombe, Bucks. Wallcharts in colour covering different aspects of wood; also timber specimens can be obtained at various prices.

Unilever Education Section, Unilever Ltd, Unilever House, London EC4. Ask for Teaching Aids Catalogue and Film Catalogue. Booklets, wallcharts free.

Van Den Berghs Ltd (Stork), Consumer Relations Manager, Kildare House, London EC4. Limited supply of booklets on margarine.

3. FIBRES

Association of Jute Spinners and Manufacturers, Kandahar House, 71 Meadowside, Dundee DD1 1EE. Teacher's notes free. Visual Aid box 37½p.

British Man Made Fibres Federation, 58 Whitworth Street, Manchester M1 6LS as above.

Cotton Board, 3 Alberton Street, Manchester 3. Publications, wallcharts, boxes of samples of cotton; filmstrips and teaching notes, films on free loan. Also free literature on cotton.

Courtaulds Ltd, Education Service, 22 Hanover Square, London W1. Charts, samples free.

The Flaxspinners' and Manufacturers' Association of Great Britain, Public Relations Office, 4 Chamber of Commerce Buildings, Dundee. Education box about flax for sale (50½p) also booklet.

I.C.I. Fibres Ltd, 68 Knightsbridge, London SW1. Notes and samples free.

International Wool Secretariat, Department of Education and Training, Wool House, Carlton Gardens, London SW1. British Wool Cloth display card, British/Scottish Wool sample book, illustrated technical books on sale at low charges.

Irish Linen Guild, Morley House, 314 Regent Street, London W1. Booklets free. Educational box 'The Story of Irish Linen', complete with samples of flax from fibre to fabric; a colour filmstrip and teachers' guide at £2.

The Silk Centre, Dorland House, 18–20 Regent Street, London SW1. Literature and samples for teachers, lecture service.

The Silk Education Service, 10 Cliffe Road, Barton on Sea, Hants. Booklets and samples – low cost.

4. GENERAL SOURCES

Central Office of Information, Circulation Section, Hercules Road, Westminster Bridge Road, London SE1. Booklet (32 pages) on the Commonwealth. Monthly Bulletins on Britain/Overseas Affairs.

Commonwealth Institute, Kensington High Street, London W 8. Free leaflets, teaching aids and film strips/slides on loan.

European Community Information Service, 23 Chesham Street, London SW1. Booklets and maps available free.

National Savings Committee, Alexandra House, Kingsway, London WC2. Free wallcharts, teaching aids and booklet dealing with money management.

Nutrition Information Centre, Vitamins Ltd, 23 Upper Mall, Hammersmith, London W6. Posters, wallcharts, folder charts and filmstrips on nutrition.

The Royal Society for the Prevention of Accidents, Terminal House, 52 Grosvenor Gardens, London SW1. Safety instruction for schoolchildren. Posters. leaflets, painting sheets, interesting story books – some free.

Royal Society for the Prevention of Cruelty to Animals, 105 Jermyn Street, London SW1. Films and filmstrips on free loan. Pamphlets, leaflets and other publications on sale or free.

U.K. Committee for UNICEF, 123 Regent Street, London W1. Booklets and catalogue of films.

UNESCO, Public Relations Division, Place Fontenoy, Paris 7. Free copies of leaflets.

United Nations Organisation, Information Centre, 14 Stratford Place, London W 1. Free copies of pamphlets and posters and films on loan.

The Universities Federation for Animal Welfare, 7a Lamb's Conduit Passage, London WC1. Filmstrips, books, posters and leaflets for sale.

War on Want, The Grove, London W5. A wealth of leaflets, booklets, posters.

5. GREAT BRITAIN

Association of Agriculture, 78 Buckingham Gate, London SW1.
Farm Study Scheme maps, photographs, statistics of farms
at home and abroad.

Commission for the New Towns (Crawley Executive), Broad-
field, Crawley, Sussex. Write for typewritten sheet on
Crawley New Towns – available in sets.

Forestry Commission, 25 Saville Row, London W1X 2AY.
Free booklets and filmstrips for purchase.

G.P.O. Regional Public Relations Officer, N.W. Postal Board,
58 Whitworth Street, Manchester M60 1DA. Excellent
wallcharts and books available.

Metropolitan Water Board, Clerks' Department, New River
Head, Roseberry Avenue, London EC1. Typescript on
'Geological Features of Board Supply Area'. Booklet
on 'Metropolitan Water Board' – source of user map in
back.

Ministry of Agriculture, Fisheries & Food, Information Division
D, Room 2A, West Whitehall Place, London SW1. Picture sets of farming in Britain (7–19 photographs in each)
on loan.

National Parks Commission, 1 Cambridge Gate, Regents Park,
London NW1. Free booklets – The National Parks of
England and Wales. Wallcharts, maps and brochures from
different areas.

North East Development Council, 20 Collingwood Street,
Newcastle 1. Available free pamphlets, statistical memor-
anda.

6. MINERALS

Alcan U.K. Ltd, Banbury Oxfordshire. Free pamphlets.

Aluminium Federation, Portland House, Stag Place, London
SW1. Publications, films and visual aids for teachers.

British Steel Corporation, 22 Kingsway, London WC1. Available free: booklets on iron and steel (good supply).

British Steel Corporation Special Steels Division, The Mount,
Broomhill, Sheffield S10 2PZ. Films on loan.

British Steel Corporation Tube Division, Administrative Officer, Corby Works, Corby, Northants. Booklets free and film catalogue.

English China Clay Co., 14 High Cross Street, St Austell, Cornwall. Free copies of booklets.

Glass Manufacturers Federation, 19 Portland Place, London W1. Booklets to teachers.

Lead Development Association, 38 Berkley Square, London W1. Free leaflets.

Rio-Tinto-Zinc, 6 St James's Square, London SW1. Free booklet.

Tin Research Institute, Fraser Road, Greenford, Middlesex. Limited supply – leaflet and perhaps a sample of tin ore.

7. POWER/FUEL

Atomic Energy Authority, Library and Information Centre, 11 Charles II Street, London SW1. Write for copies of booklets.

B.P. Oil Co. Ltd, Eaking, Nottinghamshire. Booklet available on one of the few British oil fields.

Electricity Council, 30 Millbank, London SW1. Booklets and posters supplied free of charge on application from teachers. Apply to the Education and Training Officer.

Gas Council, 59 Bryanston Street, Marble Arch, London W1A 2AZ. Not as liberal as formerly. Only a few low cost aids.

Institute of Petroleum Information Service, 61 New Cavendish Street, London W1M 8AR. Booklets available now to teaching staff only.

Mobil Oil Co. Ltd, Caxton House, Westminster, London SW1. Booklets for teachers.

National Coal Board, Hobart House, Grosvenor Place, London SW1. Available free—booklets, maps and charts; films on loan.

North Western Gas Board, Chief Home Service Adviser, Welman House, Altrincham, Cheshire. Booklets, films on loan.

Shell International Petroleum Co. Ltd, Shell Centre, London

SE1. A catalogue of aids for the teachers. (Shell International Educational Service, Shell Centre.)

Shell Mex and B.P. Ltd, Shell-Mex House, Strand, London WC2. Wall charts available.

Snowy Mountains H.E.P. Authority, Australia House, Strand, London WC2. Write for map/leaflet and list of other material.

8. THE SEA

British Transport Docks, Melbury House, Melbury Terrace, London NW1. Series of free leaflets or booklets on:

Garston Docks (Liverpool)	Grangemouth Docks
Lowestoft Harbour	Ayr Harbour
Fleetwood Docks	King's Lynn Docks
Hull	Hartlepools Dock
Grimsby – illustrated booklet	Plymouth Dock
S. Wales Ports (book)	Southampton

Glasgow: Clyde Navigation Trust, 16 Robertson Street, Glasgow C2. Issue a small brochure plus a list of cargo services from Glasgow.

Herring Industry Board, 1 Glenfinlas Street, Edinburgh 3. Free publications and film-strips; details from Information Officer. Two wallcharts from Educational Productions Ltd, East Ardsley, Wakefield, Yorks.

Manchester Ship Canal Co., Ship Canal House, King Street, Manchester M2 4WX. Free booklets and maps. Films on loan.

Mersey Docks and Harbour Board, Pierhead, Liverpool 3. Write for free copies of: Mersey Docks Annual Report (illustrated booklet); Port of Liverpool Shipping Guide; Leaflet map of Port of Liverpool.

Ministry of Agriculture, Fisheries & Food, Fisheries Division Room 518, East Whitehall Place, London SW1. Write for information.

Port of Bristol Authority, Queens Square, Bristol 1. Write for free copies of: The Port: Facts and Figures. Port Official Handbook.

Port of Hull Development Corporation, Hull. Write for free booklets and statistical sheets.

Port of London Authority, P.R.O. P.O. Box 242, Trinity Square, London EC3. Write for list of Visual Aids, booklets, filmstrips for sale.

Shipbuilders National Association, 21 Grosvenor Place, London SW1. Booklets and leaflets.

Southampton Harbour Board, Town Quay, Southampton. Very useful typescript and map of the Port.

White Fish Authority, Lincolns Inn Chambers, 3 Cursitor Street, London EC4. Free booklet (any number of copies) – 'Fish from the Sea to the Table'. Wallchart of fishing grounds/types of fish.